# BUILDING FUTURE GENERATIONAL WEALTH

YVONNE FACEY

# TABLE OF CONTENTS

INTRODUCTION ............................................................ 5

CHAPTER 1 WHY REAL ESTATE IS STILL A GREAT INVESTMENT ................................................ 9

CHAPTER 2 HOW TO MAKE INCOME PROPERTY AFFORDABLE .......................................................... 24

CHAPTER 3 ADVANTAGE AND DISADVANTAGE OF OWNING AN INCOME PROPERTY ................. 38

CHAPTER 4 MULTIPLE STREAM OF INCOME .. 51

CHAPTER 5 THE KEYS TO ASSISTING RENTAL PROPERTY OWNERS SET UP AND MANAGE THEIR PROPERTIES MORE EFFECTIVELY ........ 56

CHAPTER 6 PROPERTY MANAGER AND OTHER SERVICES ................................................................. 132

CHAPTER 7 BE YOUR OWN BEST FINANCIAL ADVISER ................................................................. 150

CONCLUSION .......................................................... 161

I believe in the dignity of labour, whether with head or hand; that the world owes no man a living but that it owes every man an opportunity to make a living.
John D. Rockefeller

Famous Quote
Knowledge Is Power.
Let's take it a step further the application of Knowledge is power.


A good man leaveth an inheritance to his children's children

# INTRODUCTION

I migrate to Canada, knew little about Real Estate, but had a desire to buy houses. At that time you could purchase one home, and use the revenue from that one to buy another one. Work hard to save my money one years had ten thousand dollars ready to buy my first home at the age of twenty. Engaged to be married at the time to a guy one year younger. Learn the hard way taking him into something that he was not ready to take on. He was living in public housing, and I am trying to make him a homeowner a dimension that was out of his comfort zone.
Use a Real Estate agent recommended by a friend told him needed a house with an apartment to rent. He got a townhouse with an unfinished basement and told me we could finish it by putting a little kitchenette in it. Spent all my saving on that house my fiancé at the time encourage me to take it.
 The Real Estate agent did not work in my best interest; he wants to make his commission from us not knowing much about Real Estate
. When we moved to the house, the fridge and stove, washer and dryer that was a part of the deal were taken out by the previous owners.

They replaced the refrigerator and stove with an old one but no washer and dryer. Contacted the lawyer regarding all the appliances told me would have to pay him money to take the previous owners to court. My fiancé was not much help, so was carrying most of the expense, and he did everything he could do to destroy it. Eventually lost it, but I never give up my dream to own Real Estate. Develop a passion for the Real Estate world every opportunity to go to a presentation would make an effort to attend, and read books.

Then 2013 took a Property Management Course and achieved a Diploma in Property Management. I also started the Real Estate course but did not complete it as yet. It remains a future goal. This book is to help others who have a desire to buy income property not to get into the trap I fell in; will have the confidence to build generational wealth. Being in business was my first love from growing up as a child and nursing my second love. My grand aunt who I grow up with and my grandfather had grocery stores and had a great interest in learning the business.

Enjoy the nursing profession, but my passion for business soar. Spoke to some of my friends about leaving Nursing to pursue my love of business. Those friends kept telling me that I was good at Nursing. I kept listening to them; it got to a place; decided to move them out of my life because they were not contributing to my success. Always strive for excellence in whatever you do.

Pursue Network Marketing Businesses; sold Portable Personal Alarm and Portable Home Alarm system, Skin Care Line.

Purchase one of the alarm for my apartment at the time, a few years later, someone tries to break into my apartment that alarm prevents them from getting into the apartment. It had work by volumetric air pressure, as the person tries to beat the lock to open, the exchange of air in the apartment triggers the alarm system, so the person had to leave. The door severely damaged a locksmith had to open the door and place a metal plate around the lock on the door to realign it.

Donald Trump purchases some of his books and read. He was a very savvy businessman and knew how to create wealth even in the downturn of the market, vast knowledge about real estate. Even doe I had lost my house, it still was a great accomplishment for me.

My desire to gain wealth is to be a problem solver in a troubled world. Some of the homeless people on the street educated had good jobs; they make the wrong turn, do not know where to turn to get back on track. Work as a nurse for a very long time in the community, hospital and nursing home interact with different level of people. Most of the time, they do not want to remain in the same situation.

One of the charities would like to sponsor; helps people in Asia; love the concept of teaching people how to fish instead of giving them a fish for a day.

They help men to get cows, goats, chickens, and women sewing machines, to build small businesses to provide for their families.

It is a perpetual (continued without intermission) law 'give, and it shall be given unto you. Microsoft founder Bill Gates and renowned investor Warren Buffett donate a significant amount of their fortune to charities. They practice the perpetual law, and they can never be in lack.

At the age of 8, went into the grocery store owned and managed by my grandaunt Lilly-bell Campbell and asked her to allow me to assist her in the store. Her reply was no because I would not know how to weight the foodstuff, e.g. rice, flour correctly. Most of the food products were not a self-package like today, had to be bag and weight on a scale. Friday' and Saturday's was the busiest time in the store, so figure if I help the customer would get served faster. Did not accept her no; make her another offer that she should pre-package frequently requested products like rice, flour. In a bag of 1 lb, 2lbs and 3lbs then would be able to help her serve, which agreed. Mathematics was my favourite subject, so eventually, she allows me to do the credit accounts for the customers who credit and pay. As a child, I did not like to ask for pocket money, found ways of making my own money by stocking my grandfather store with eggs when staying with him. I was always an entrepreneur from a young age.

# CHAPTER 1 WHY REAL ESTATE IS STILL A GREAT INVESTMENT

The most significant fortunes made in Real Estate dates back in history, and still today. The monarch from England they had controlled a substantial number of countries through Real Estate (lands) and make a considerable amount of their wealth. Real Estate is still the way to create long-term secure generational wealth. Real Estate markets profoundly influenced by local events, jobs, industry, and government at the local level. You are not limited to buy Real Estate only in the country, State, or Providence you have your principle resident. You can purchase it in other foreign countries. Some foreign countries will allow you to buy Real Estate properties in their country as non- resident cash. Cannot get a mortgage from them to purchase. New York City, the City of Toronto, Vancouver Canada, is very expensive to buy Real Estate, but those properties are still selling because the demand outweighs the supply. The demographics of people attracted to those areas pushes the price up, e.g., the wealthy immigrant, business people.

When you look at Florida USA, the supply and demands are different because it more appeals to the retirement population, you can find reasonable properties to purchase. No matter the fluctuation in the market, it is still the best investment. When there is fluctuation in the real estate market. You are not selling your income property. So it would not affect you; it is still making money for you.

Income property is the best investment to have in your retirement portfolio, over Mutual Funds, Stocks, and Bonds. All of those other investment has its value, but they still have limitation. Invest for your retirement in an RRSP (Registered Retirement Saving Plan) the money is lock-in. If you redeem a small amount of the funds ($5000) each time, you are tax at a lower rate. You redeem large amount ($10,000) you will be tax at a higher tax bracket. You have an Income Property earning $2500, and the expenses on it are $1200, gaining a profit of $1300 every month when you retire that income is still coming in. After paying off the mortgage that income property profit gain will increase to about $2000 per month. It's a business so you can claim the allowable business expenses on your income tax. You can pass down that income property, and to your children, they can, in turn, do the same, and the generational cycle continues. Your Canadian Pension can only transfer to a spouse. If you are from other countries, you would have to check what pension benefits are there at retirement.

Real Estate investments facilitate different ways in which profits made, e.g., lease options, sandwich leases and flipping property. Lease options also called lease-to-own and rent-to-own. An income property that fully rented is known as a turn-key property. Sandwich leases option if you purchase a property through lease option, you can then rent the property out to another tenant-buyer. It is called a sandwich leases option. Flipping House is buying a rundown property renovate it in a short time frame and resell it. You purchase at a lower price and sell at a higher price value. It is a quick profit strategy sometimes used by Real Estate Investor.

The properties they are buying or older houses, and foreclosures in-house flipping business they can acquire these properties relatively cheap and make a higher profit.

There are three ways to make money under the sandwich leases option. Monthly cash flow- Rent the property to your tenant-buyer at a higher rate than what you agree to pay the seller. Option payment- when you sell to your tenant-buyer, you can make money on the option payment.

Sale profits- Is the difference between what you have agreed to pay the seller and what the tenant-buyer has agreed to pay you. Other investments do not give the same leverage as Real Estate investments, e.g., mutual funds, the stock market you pay 100% of your own money.

In Real Estate, you can leverage other people money to invest. RRSP some financial institution will lend a small loan to buy Mutual Funds because it is a lock-in plan.

Leverage is the most potent instrument in Real Estate. You are using other people's money to buy Real Estate and build long-term generational wealth. Other people money allows you to control a lot more Real Estate asset with a smaller amount of money out of your pocket. The banks and other lenders will give you money to purchase Real Estate classified as a secure investment.

The property owner controls 100% of the asset value, with only 5% to 20% of your cash invested. The advantages of owning a rental property are tax advantages, property appreciation, and earning rental cash flow. Some of the tax advantages are a huge benefit, e.g., rental and management expense deductions; insurance for rental property is deductible.

Your portion of the utility bills you pay not the tenant portion, marketing, and advertising expense deductions. Always make sure you do a home inspection on the property you purchase. It can prevent you a lot of headache at the end of the day, to rule out all the potential problems.

Income suites can increase the value of your home. In many ways bringing extra income, raise the resale price, increase potential buyers interest set an affordability tone as to when housing prices are very high. In some cases, non-approved mortgage for marginal buyers having a legal rental suite can reclassify them into a mortgage qualified. The bank takes into consideration the extra income they will generate from the rental suite to qualify them. Income properties many times pay for themselves as the unit increase in value over time. Income property can cause multiple offers for the seller, which can mean a higher selling price. I would discourage anyone who bought a house with an income suite not to destroy it because you are reducing the value of your property.

Let's look at this scenario; when you bought the property just for you and your family to live. Several years later, situation change, e.g., a divorce, so the loss of one income, loss of a job, children move away to college/university. Paying for children educations still, have a mortgage on the property. The bank shows up first of the month looking for the mortgage payment; children tuition has to pay you still have that one or two-bedroom rental suite. You could rent it out, bringing anywhere from $900.00 to about $1200.00 per month. Many people get caught in the emotions of the now syndrome instead of looking at the long-term benefits.

Do not buy Real Estate with feelings always have a long-term goal to deal with a what-if, the bank owns that house for a period of fifteen, twenty-five or thirty years. It is yours to live in, decorates it however you like. Do not pay your mortgage payments for two to three months; the Bank will show up and terminate your occupancy. The bank does not care about the situation that causes you to be unable to pay the mortgage; he wants his payments.

When you are buying a property as an investment always consider the area to activate your purchasing power. The location is still the key to defining the types of tenants, the price you can charge, the accessibility to public transit. Demographic of people drive up or reduce the rent you can charge; you live in an area with high unemployment, transportation problems. You are at a higher risk of renting out your income property. When looking to purchase an investment property understand the municipality bylaws for multi-unit homes, these bylaws vary. Some municipalities' bylaws forbidden income suites in family homes.

If you had bought the property with a suite, you are allowed to keep it (grandfathered the property), but you are not approved to build a new one. The municipality restricts income suites or more in the suburban area. To maintain low population density; to encourage new construction and therefore capitalizations of more property tax potential.

If you are building or renovating an income suite, you need to know the actual cost and leave extra contingency funds for the unexpected repairs. Soundproofing your units is an asset to long-term occupancy. Fireproofing your units is very important to make it a legal income suite.

Under the fire code, an income suite is required to have the second exit that will provide an escape route if the main entrance blocked. A window can use as the second escape route, but it must be large enough for a big size person to go through. If it is too high for a person to climb through during an emergency, consider building a window bench that has multiple functions as a storage and a bench to climb on. You have more than one suite in a property. You must have interconnected smoke alarms system that as one goes off in one unit, the alarms in other units will also trigger. There is also the interconnected smoke alarms combined with carbon monoxide detectors that serve a dual purpose and could be more cost-effective.

Some people will encourage property owners not to put bathtubs in their income suite or remove the existing tub. When a tenant has a tub bath, they use more water. I tend to be in disagreement with that logic because a person can take a shower and use the same amount of water. The negative impact it can have on an income suite you had a two-bedroom apartment a couple live in for about three years.

They are going to have a baby, but the bathroom only has a shower, not a tub. The new addition to their family will let them leave to find more suitable accommodation to meet their needs. You now have to find new tenants that you will have to get acquainted with, the cost to paint and clean up for new tenants, just because of the lack of a tub. Always make sure you can recoup the investment it cost you to renovate the suite within three to five years to gain affordability. Having an income suite in your home or an investment property increase your income that can change your tax bracket.

Home insurance cost might increase add a rider that will protect you against loss of, rental income, e.g., against flood and fire. Increase in your home value might reflect an increase in property tax. Some property owners/landlord might ask should I rent my income suite furnished /unfurnished.

I am not a big supporter of renting an income suite furnished unless it is executive rentals or student rentals due to sanitation problems. You can charge more for a furnished suite but can cost you a lot more to maintain because of the turnover rate of executive rentals or student rentals. All tenants are not the same, some or very clean and others do not care; one of the significant problems you can occur is bedbugs. If you have bedbugs, you might have to throw out all the furniture and purchase a new set.

After each client vacates the furnished suite invest in a steamer and steam clean mattress, sofa it is cloth material, if you have carpet.

The residential Real Estate is still the best investment for wealth building. When buying the residential Real Estate, it is better to obtain an investment property instead of just a single home dwelling. Having a house that you can live in and also rent a part of it, it will help to fund your mortgage. A house with more than one washroom and a second kitchen is an excellent asset for resale and often increase the value. Sometimes buying a home in a school, hospital, train station, fire station zone sometimes can be a bit difficult for resale due to constant noise caused by these facilities. House with a swimming pool sometimes can be difficult for resale and make the high property risk for the possibility of drowning. A one-bedroom condominium apartment can be complicated for resale.

It is better to purchase a one-bedroom with a den or up. Having an apartment in a condominium or your private home than rent it as an executive rental, you can gain a good return and your investment. Can remain for a more extended period empty, in comparison to renting it month to month.

# RENT TO OWN

Rent to own or lease to own option give people who would like to own but unable to go through the regular channel to purchase with a down payment and getting a mortgage. Most contracts have an upfront payment clause ranging from about $5000 and up that is non-refundable if the purchasing buyer refused to purchase the property at the end of the agreed terms. In the traditional way of buying Real Estate, you make an offer on the property, and the seller accepts the buyer offer put down a deposit. If the buyer did not retain a mortgage for the property to complete the purchase, their deposit is non-refundable. For the person who wants to acquire income property but does not want to be a landlord, this is a good option for your rent to own property. For the rent to own seller of the property, you save on Real Estate Agent commission that you would typically pay them. To find you a buyer because you already have the buyer living in your house. For the rent, to own buyer, it allows them to check out the neighbourhood if it is the right area. Also what it entails to own a piece of Real Estate and if you decide to buy it, you do not have to move. If you had tenants, you do not have to uproot them if you still need that income.

As a rent to own property owner gives your potential home buyer an incentive to want to purchase that property at the end of the terms agreed.

Offer small cashback from each month rent towards the option to buy, if they are buying at the end of the agreement. Some lease to own contract can have where the potential buyer responsible for all necessary repairs and some will have a percentage amount. Essential maintenance of a stove not working, leaky faucet, but nothing to do with structural repairs. Potential home buyer, you can request a clause in the agreement to have the ability to rent out a portion of the property while living in it to work for you. To give you stronger purchasing power at the end of the terms. You rent a house and have full control of it; you can rent out a portion of it to generate extra revenue. To put towards your option to purchase at the end of the lease agreement for one to three years. You also have full or partial responsibility for the maintenance and utilities to pay for it. If a pipe broke, it is your job to call a plumber and fund part, or the full repairs or the property owner fund a portion base on the agreement. Some property owner will save a small percentage from the rent to give back to you towards the purchase option. You pay $1600 per month for rent they might save $200 per month for three years total $7200 to go toward your down payments.

If it was a three bedrooms house with a basement, you could rent out the upper level living in the basement base on the amount of space you need. The three rooms could rent individually at about $400-500 each or to one family $1400-$1500 per month. You would have to only pay about $200 per month for your share of the rent plus utilities. Utilities cost you about $500-$650 per month, so from that $1600, you have a saving of $950, you could save about $800 towards your down payment each month and the other $150 save for any repairs. For a lease agreement of three years, you would save a total of $28,800 towards the down payment and save for repairs is $5400. What you save towards down payment $28,800 plus the property owners give you $7200 give you a total of $36000. The owner will only give you the $7200 if, at the end of the lease, you still want to activate the option to purchase. At the end of the lease agreement, you can activate the option to purchase or decline the option to purchase, but you still come out with $28,800 saving.

The property owner also gained $57,600 and did not have to pay any maintenance or utilities regarding the agreement. The owner had a mortgage of $800 per month for the three years $28,800, the utilities you paid $23,400, repairs $3500.

It is what the owner gain look like rent $57,600 plus the utilities you paid $23,400, repairs $3500 a total of $84,500. After the owner subtracts the mortgage form, the gain of three years still leaves with a total of $55,700.

 If you activate the option to purchase the owner gain is $55,700 subtract your $7200 to go towards your down payment the total profit is $48,500 plus the purchasing price of the house. Sometimes people talk others out of exercising the option to rent to own or lease to own because they think it is a rip off because the property owner is the only winner. After all the detail information given to you make your decisions based on facts and not assumption or hearsay.

You can rent a three bedrooms apartment for the same $1600, but you do not get the same size space, most of the time you cannot rent out any of the room. You would have paid your landlord for the same three years a total $57,600, with no saving towards a down payment, no option to purchase. Pay your mortgage biweekly instead of monthly can pay off your mortgage faster. An open mortgage is suitable so on the anniversary of each year you can pay a lump sum of money on it to reduce the amortization period.

Sometimes people buy houses with too much-unused space not use or need, the bigger the area, the more expensive the utilities will be to maintain it. The house should be working for you instead of you working for it. Go back in history many of enormous fortunes have been made in Real Estate and still today. The commercial Real Estate is another good investment. Can be more challenging to get it to lease or rent and see a quick rate of return on your money.

A better commercial Real Estate to invest in a property with a rental apartment. You can rent it out and gain some income while you wait to get the store rented. Commercial Real Estate with multiple units to rent or lease, is a great asset when fully occupied.

Executive Rental is another type of Income Property, but it is for the more season investors that have money. If it sits for two months are more not rented, they do not have to worry about paying the mortgage because they are financially comfortable. You can purchase a condo and use it as Executive Rental stay ranging from a month, two months or more. You can earn a lot of money on Executive Rental if you have the right connections and know-how. To offer some extra bonuses like cleaning service weekly, bi-weekly or monthly.

A word of advice to all potential property owners when you make an offer on the property the appliances that are a part of the agreement takes note of the serial numbers.

Institute an inspection clause in the contract for the day before or on the day of the deal closing. The owners remove any appliances that should remain then refused to close the deal. Things to do to increase the value of your property are painting, new flooring, building an income suite, renovating kitchen and bathrooms. Home prices go up every year, so it is a positive way to generate equity.

# CHAPTER 2 HOW TO MAKE INCOME PROPERTY AFFORDABLE

Multiple streams of income make income property more affordable. When I said, multiple incomes does not always mean taking on a second job; an income suite is also another source of income. To the property owner that does not want to be a landlord or do not wish to have any tenant living in their home; you have a right to choose. Let examine the facts you are a single parent take on a second job, never able to spend time with your children. You cannot control what they do; one child begins to hang with unfavourable friends. The second job put you in a higher tax bracket. Wherein which the income from your home would generate business income which is tax differently; business expenses could be claimed. There are different types of wealth, i.e., the wealth of knowledge, a wealth of skills, financial wealth, and a wealth of success. Wealth – (1) abundance of possessions or resources (2) abundant supply profusion (3) all property that has the money or an exchange value; also all objects or resources that have economic value. SYN: fortune, property, substance, worth. There are only two classes of people, the more impoverished class and the more affluent class.

Some people refer to themselves as middle class. That does not fit in technically anywhere. Some are about two paycheques away from bankruptcy. They try to keep up with the Joneses. So everything is max out living on a credit card, to maintain that high-end lifestyle.

What is the income middle-class people earn? Financial wealth: Having substantial financial resources, and there is no strict definition of how much one needs to have to be wealthy. It refers to one with significantly more assets than liabilities. Wealth is a measure of the value of all of the assets of worth owned by any one person, e.g., companies, properties stocks, and bonds. Wealth is found by taking the total market value of all the physical and tangible assets of the entity and then subtracting all debts to know the individuals net worth. Measurable wealth typically excludes intangible or nonmarketable assets such as human capital and social capital. Some people want to be called wealthy, but they are rich and usually struggle to find the balance between having money and being wealthy. Rich defined as someone who has accumulated enough to purchase the comfort of a luxurious nature above that of the ordinary people in a group, city, and society. Someone who has attained wealth has more above the group of rich people and achieves a new level of luxury.

A wealth of Knowledge: It is such an essential parameter in one's life.

If you acquire knowledge, you will excel in your job, business, profession, and life. It is the most important without the wealth of knowledge it is impossible to achieve your dreams and aspiration. If you are unable to purchase an income property by yourself, you can use a joint venture that is when you go into partnership with others. Joint venture: To establish or enter a joint venture or partnership. Two or more persons want to buy a house, but they cannot afford to purchase individually.

They can use a joint venture, where they can pool their money together and buy a home. In a joint venture using a lawyer to draft up your agreement, make sure it has a good buy out clause in the case of one person after a period a time wants out. In this case, key person insurance is good to have.

You might not know anyone to do a joint venture with then starts a joint venture club; sometimes other people are in the same position as you. Open it to all different income level of people; some might not have money to invest at the beginning but aspire than to their success. Develop a program to help those people to reach their goals. Read the book The Wealthy Barber many years ago, here is a barber who cuts people hair. A lot of successful men sat in his barber chair and shared different topics such as stocks, real estate, insurance. He would listen to them and make notes and invest, and he became very wealthy.

There is a movie where the chauffeur as he drove around his boss who likes to talk about stocks and other investments. He listens to him and begins to buy stocks from his small income and became a millionaire, without his boss knowledge. One of my favourites books is the Law of Success, where Napoleon Hill talks about Henry Ford, John D Rockefeller, Dale Carnegie, who were from an impoverished upbringing. They would spend time with other like-minded people in a mastermind group inspire each other. They all became very wealthy men. If you want to become successful, be an aspired reader, read books on areas of interest, e.g., in the field of science technology, investments, other successful men, and women. A millionaire read a book per week; the average person reads a book per year.

Millionaire knows one of the keys to success is through self-thought. The school was designed to refine our mind, establish a way of life and how to relate to people. The intellect of the mind might never correctly rate from college or university. School teaches us how to be a worker at a job; it does not facilitate knowledge of how to built wealth. Having an education is excellent, but some time to get to your predestined life, you need to be self-thought. Microsoft founder Bill Gates did not finish school; he is the second richest man in the world.

Thirty years later they gave him a Doctorate Degree. I recently got a copy of The Millionaire Mindset How Ordinary People Can Create Extraordinary Income by Gerry Robert the simplicity of it makes it a masterpiece. He talks about how his financial mentor changes his mindset from poverty to a millionaire. He teaches about multiple sources of income the rich and powerful always knew about wealth creation. People should have some affiliation to your club even if there are not members of your club. Real Estate Lawyers, Bankers, Accountants, Real Estate Agents, Construction Companies, Moving Companies, Cleaning Companies, Property Managers. You could invite them to give a speech and any subject related to their field of expertise. Through your club, you could aspirer a single mother on social assistance to turn her life around and be a property owner. By giving her jobs to clean all the income properties that members bought, and they pay her just as if they had hired a cleaning company to do the job. Then show her how to save some of the funds towards being an income property owner. Two income family with two children, wife, earns $2000 and husband $3000 per month after tax and renting an apartment both drive high-end cars. What could this couple do to become a property owner, reduce their lifestyle, live on one person income and save the other person income for a down payment on a piece of Real Estate?

For instance, live off the husband income and save the wife income. They would save $24,000 for the year.

Buying property tax liens residential, commercial and undeveloped land that under foreclosure for property tax. A tax lien is when a landowner fails to pay the taxes on their property. Then the city or county in which the property located has the authority to place a lien on the property. Lien is a legal claim, and the property cannot be sold or refinanced until taxes paid and the lien removed. A tax lien certificate created by the municipality that reflects the amount that owed on the property plus any interest or penalties that are due. These certificates are then auctioned off and subsequently issued to the highest bidding investor. The auctions may hold in a physical setting or online. In Canada, we cannot buy property liens, but you can purchase them through the USA. The city or county paid their police, firefighter, and teachers with funds from the property taxes. You can buy property liens on residential, commercial and undeveloped land.

You can contact the city or county treasurer to find out when, where and how the next auction will hold. Each city or county has a different rate of return of property tax liens. After the lien is purchased, they inform the homeowner and allow them to pay the bill with the interest and penalties. If they settle the debt, you will receive a payment of the purchasing price and interest.

You can hold a property tax lien for property for year or more. Although property tax liens can yield substantial rates of interest, investors need to do their homework before starting buying these liens. Many years ago, I went to one of Donald Trump meeting a wealth-building as the presenter talking about how to buy property liens in the USA. Canada we do not have such a program. In the USA the county uses the property taxes to pay Policemen, Firemen. So when a property owner does not pay their taxes, they put a lien on the property, and people from another country can purchase that lien. The county will notify the owner that the lien sold and the amount owed to the lienholder with interest. And the time frame they have to pay it, or the lien holder can take the full position of the property. The presenter said something so profound "if you take ownership of the property and a family lives in it do not evict them. Allow them to stay there until they can improve their situation, let them pay what they can afford. Here he is practising the power of sowing and reaping.

Here is a real scenario where this person let's call her Susan had an income suite in her home. Discourage to rent it by her retired parents living on pension their income very small. The income suite could yield about $700 -$800 per month. Susan income was not sufficient and short most of the months to pay her bills and keep using credit cards to offset the shortfall.

Create massive debts and several times have to consolidate it into the mortgage. Is Susan paying down her debt? "No" mortgage payments became larger. Let use Susan income suite for $700 per month for one year would gain $8400 in income.

# SOME THINGS THAT CAN AFFECT AFFORDABILITY IN REAL ESTATE

Some of the things that affect affordability in attaining Real Estate. Not having good money sense, bad spending habits, and generational cycle. The same way how their parents handle finances, they repeat the sequence from generation to generation. Some people blame it on not having enough money. The truth is that even if you give some people a million-dollar, they still would not able to acquire a property. They would go and buy all the furniture's to put in a house but did not purchase the home. It is called putting the cart before the horse, meaning the cart is in front of the horse, the horse will not be able to pull it.

The bride to be "I want my dream wedding" it's my day, worked two jobs for two years to save $25,000 or more for a wedding. The optimum word in that statement is "day" a singular tense. In that day the wedding ends, and the marriage starts with empty accounts moving into the future.

Have no tangible investment like a piece of Real Estate but will go to death to have this dream wedding. That dream is a wild and vain fantasy for one day when it is all over having difficulty in paying your bills. The number one reason couples' fights are over money. Attended a wedding that was over three hundred guests, the groom mother says she is going to give him a wedding he will never forget, and it was so. Five years later they were still paying for the wedding. If you have some tangible investments, have the money without going into debt or overworking yourself to pay for it. At the end, not cash poor then go for your dream wedding.

Let me talk to the fashionista. I love to dress and look smart, but it is how to do it. Remember travelling to New York was going for a brother wedding; the first time would meet my sister-in-law. Dress in a lovely dress while checking someone approach me, and ask if I was a government official. I volunteered on a very prestigious award committee in Toronto for three years. A Part of the core committee where the planning and the process took place, also Volunteer Coordinator for two years.

One year wear a beautiful orange evening gown when the City of Toronto Premier arrive. A security person calls me thought I was the one to welcome him.

Present to a committee to sponsor a youth table to bring disadvantaged youth to the event. Dress business casual; it was not about my dress why they agree to sponsor a youth table.

It was how I eloquently explain to the committee about the Awards Event, and as an organization, we begin to ask for sponsors to bring disadvantaged youths to the event. It was to show those youths where they are in life they can change their situation. If they work hard enough; one day they could be an award recipient too. As fashion guru would say have a few elegant pieces of jewellery, so decide to buy a beautiful diamond ring original price was over three thousand. After a year it was reduce purchased it for $1800 and the appraisal value at $5000. Many years later check if wanted to sell it what the jeweller would pay me for it $250. Some of the university professor's shops at second-hand stores but find beautiful clothing and some designer's brands. Fashionista (informal) a person who follows trends in the fashion industry obsessively and strives continually to adopt the latest fashions. Dressing for success is still essential, but you do not have to break the bank to look great.

If you are a person who goes to work five days per week and buy lunch every day, it cost $10.00 per day. You spend $50.00 for the week a month $200.00 just for lunch. Take lunch using a budget of $100.00 per month to make meal having your vegetables, fruits.

For the year you could save $1200.00. Your original cost of buying lunch for the year was $2400.00. Oprah Winfrey is a wealthy lady, but she took lunch to work to save money.

A significant percentage of people do not own a piece of Real Estate but drive high-end cars living in a rental property. Cars depreciate as soon as you drove it off the lot. The money you are using to finance that high-end car cut it in half and put some aside to purchase a piece of Real Estate. Consider having a tangible piece of Real Estate before the high-end vehicle. A piece of Real Estate that goes up in value. The reality is you cannot live in your car. If you talk to most successful millionaires would tell you they do not go out and buy a high-end vehicle at the beginning of building wealth. If they do is not a brand new one but a few years old, so they do not have to pay all the cost that goes into buying a new one.

The goal of the rich is how to achieve more wealth, looking for their next business venture. A rich person and a wealthy person do not carry the same status.

The rich person wakes up to an alarm clock to go to work to make that six-figure income, working for someone else or having their own business. A wealthy person does not wake up by an alarm clock move at his or her leisure.

They tap into the power of residual income, where their money works for them, not them working for it. Through Real Estate, investments, owning huge cooperations with people working for then, through inheritance. Rich people have a high possibility of running out of money by a stock market crash or loss of job or business and not having the ability to leave generational wealth.

Wealthy people, on the other hand, even with the stock market crash, loss of some businesses will still have the ability to leave wealth to many generations and again would not run out of money. If some people take stock of their life, they can exercise power to cut cost and achieve that income property that they think is so farfetched.

In the movie, Pursuit of Happiness was base on a true story; the father and son were playing basketball. He told his son never let anyone tell you cannot do anything. Do not have to be doctors and Lawyers to achieve Real Estate. It does not matter what level you are in life you can achieve Real Estate by yourself or through a partnership.

An associate said her mother makes this statement "she did the job that no one wanted cleaning houses." Now she owns a house and a Camper Trailer bus to go and travel.

A lot of big building we see today there funded by many different sources. Many people do not talk about the builder's fund where a regular person could have $5000.00.

Put it into a building fund to gain some interest on their money as a shareholder but not as a property owner. These are some of the option to help you achieve that down payment to fund your income property. Henry Ford did not invent the automobile or the assembly line; he developed and manufactured the first automobile that much middle-class Americans could afford it.

Ford converted the automobile from an expensive curiosity into a practical conveyance, which would profoundly impact the twentieth century. Ford introduction of the Model T automobile revolutionized transportation in American industry. In 1913, Henry Ford's team reinvented manufacturing by introducing the moving assembly line. It worked well, but the workers hated the jobs. They quit almost as quickly as they complete training.

On January 5, 1914, he announced double workers pay and shorten the workday. Instead of $2.34 for nine hours, most workers would make $5.00 for eight hours. Manufacturers said it was crazy and socialist and cost Ford 10 million dollars that year alone. But the very next day, 10,000 people flocked to Highland Park with a loud uproar for jobs, and turnover dropped drastically.

Workers entered the middle class and could afford to buy the cars they built.

Henry Ford became a hero to millions. As the owner of the Ford Motor Company, he became one of the richest and best-known people in the world.
You might be wondering why I am using a car story, and this book is about Real Estate buying Income Property. The key component in this story and the topic is affordability. Henry Ford increases his employee's income to give them the ability to afford the cars they built.
If you want to purchase an income property, you have to make the necessary adjustment in your life to make it attainable.
In conclusion, here are some tips to make that income property more affordable. If you do not have a large size family, you could live in the basement apartment. Rent out the upstairs that bring in more rent, stop leaving those rooms that call guest rooms for people who occasionally visit. It is called wasted space, rent it and capitalized extra revenue. A lot of people own a home and will say that they do not have money to buy an income property but sits on "dead money."
What do I mean by dead money that basement that you said it is a Recreation room but
occasionally use. That can generate income but not using it to its full potential earning income? Always put a clause in your contract to inspect the property one more time before the closing date the day before or the same day will save you a lot of stress in the end.

# CHAPTER 3 ADVANTAGE AND DISADVANTAGE OF OWNING AN INCOME PROPERTY

The advantage of owning income property is earning positive cash flow from rental income. Building generational wealth, control more Real Estate asset by leveraging other people's money, pay-down principles on mortgage faster. Increase the ability to make their mortgage payments. Add value to their home and force appreciation.

The disadvantage of owning income property is dealing with difficult tenants, vacant rental unit, dealing with emergencies in a rental property. As a property owner, you will have more responsibilities including maintaining the property, fixing and paying for it.

## WHAT IS POSITIVE AND NEGATIVE CASH FLOW

Cash flow is total rental property income minus operating expenses. Total rental income collected each month minus paying all expenses, e.g. property taxes, insurance, mortgage, repairs, utilities.

The balance left over is positive cash flow. Negative cash flow is when there is a zero balance after paying all expense or has to add money to the total property income to cover expenses.

# CREDIT

Knowing your credit score is very important. Having a good credit score dictates your interest rate and which lenders will lend to you when shopping for your mortgage. Your credit score does not influence your likelihood of getting a mortgage as much as your monthly income. A bad credit score will cause you to pay a premium for your mortgage.

# DIFFERENT TYPES OF DEBT

Unsecured debt is a credit card, a line of credit and personal loan. Secured debt is a loan takes to lease or purchase a car. Failure to make your payments a lender can repose your vehicle. Consumer debt arising from the purchase of goods and services borrow money from a lender other than the government.

These are the factors affecting your credit and their weight:

Credit history -------------------------15 percent
Payment history --------------------35 percent

Inquiries ------------------------------10 percent

Credit types --------------------------10 percent

Outstanding credit balance -------30 percent

These numbers on your credit report mean the following

RO – Too new for a creditor to rate

R1- Consumer is current on his/her obligations

R2- Consumer is one payment late (30-60 days overdue)

R3- Consumer is two payments late (60-90 days overdue)

R4- Consumer is three payments late (90-120 days overdue)

R5- Consumer is four payments late (a minimum of 120 days overdue)

R7- Consumer is making payments under a debt management plan with a credit counselling agency.

R9- Creditor has written then account off as a bad debt (150 to 180 days overdue)

The higher your credit score, the more you are considered a good credit risk.

You should apply for your credit report at least two times per year from Transunion and Equifax.

Make sure the credit report you apply for has your credit score on it.

Credit rating is a numbers game assigned to items that appear on your credit report.

You can detect inaccurate information, a creditor's failure to update payments information, settlement, an outstanding account and fraud.

A debtor does have the right to put a consumer statement on their credit report of about a hundred words to explain their delinquent debts. Caused by loss of job, divorce, illness and unable to work.

Many people are not aware of the term "utilization rate" this is the percentage of a debtor credit card balance versus debtor credit card limit.

For a debtor to maintain or increase their credit score their balance on any one personal credit card or loan should not exceed the utilization rate of 35%. If a debtor utilization rate is consistently higher than 35 percent, credit bureaus will see them be high risk for credit.

If a debtor can have utilization rate 35% or less, it is considered an indicator they are a good manager of their credit. They, therefore, fit the profile of someone who will be able to repay their debt.

If you are using the credit card for business, the debtor utilization rate can be as high as 75%.

Have three revolving credit lines and up but no more than ten and spread your balance over all the cards to maintain your utilization rate of 35% on each card.

A person sometimes goes into the mall a department store offers them a credit card to get 10% off their purchase on the spot. It is not a great deal because new inquiries are hard inquiries that count against your credit score.

Hard inquiries reduce your credit scores. If you need to repair your credit score use two secured credit cards after about 6 to 18 months of building a good record, and then ask the bank to change it to an unsecured credit card.

Have one instalment loan and no more than three and instalment loan that is great for your credit score requires the first payment within 30 days after purchasing the item.

The type of instalment loans that hurt your credit score delays payments. You buy a sofa at the furniture store and do not pay until six months later. This type of instalment loan suggests the credit bureau that you are under financial strain and do not have the funds to make immediate payments.

The interest rates on the sofa will be much higher; it is better you save and purchase it six months later cash.

When applying for credit cards, apply the second to the third week of the month, and if applying for more than one card, apply for them at the same time.

Do not cut up your credit cards because it does not affect your credit history.

Your Score Credit score range from 300-900.

Eight hundred and above –Excellent: You are considered in the top percentage of those most favourable to lenders.

700-799 –Very Good: You are considered a low risk to borrow money.

660-699 –Acceptable: You won't necessarily receive the best interest rates on loans.

620-659-Weak: If you can obtain a loan, you will pay much higher interest, and your loan term may be less than ideal.

Below 620-Bad: You are considered very high risk by lenders and may default on loans.

MORTGAGES

A mortgage considered conventional when the borrower has a down payment of 20 percent or more of the property value.

A mortgage is termed a high ratio when the borrower has less than 20 percent down payment. Higher interest rates and mortgage insurance are frequent costs connected with a higher ratio mortgage.

An open mortgage the borrower can modify the particulars of the mortgage before the term ended.

A closed mortgage means the borrower must stick with the original details of the mortgage until the term and condition ended they cannot modify it.

A fixed or variable mortgage refers to the type of interest rate on your mortgage.

A fixed-rate mortgage has an interest rate that does not change for the duration of the mortgage term.

A variable mortgage or adjustable-rate mortgage the interest rate float, with what is called the prime rate or prime. Prime is a rate set by the central bank that allows the government to control economic factors like inflation.

An assumable mortgage can be transferred from the seller to the buyer at the sale of the property.

A portable mortgage can be carried over by the mortgagor from one property to another.

A mortgage loan a loan secured by real property use of a mortgage which evidences the existence of the loan and the encumbrance of that reality.

A mortgage is the most affordable kind of loan because you can use your property to secure your loan.

Lenders usually offer more affordable rates because they have something to hold on to in case you fail to pay your debt.

Planning to get a home loan, be mindful of some essential things.

First, you should consider your budget before inquiring about a mortgage.

Make sure that your money can pay your monthly payments to avoid incurring penalties.

It can also help you to prevent missing payment deadlines and to lose your property.

To plan your mortgage budget efficiently, shop around for mortgages that have affordable rates.

Choose a credible lender that can provide you with an excellent loan rate.

Ask for free quotes from different lenders to choose your ideal mortgage program.

The second thing that you should do is to plan your finances carefully after acquiring a mortgage.

It can help you to spend the money that you borrowed wisely.

People use their mortgages to purchase a new house or renovate those that they already have. Lastly, you must analyze the terms and conditions of your home loan product. You have to learn how your mortgage rate works and how you should pay your loan. It is advisable to check for your interest rate to know your monthly payments and study your amortization period to learn your total mortgage costs.

A variable-rate mortgage, adjustable-rate mortgage (ARM), or tracker mortgage is a mortgage loan with the interest rate on the note periodically. Adjusted based on an index which reflects the cost to the lender of borrowing on the credit markets

The most common ARMs are seven years, five years and three years.

At the end of the period, it is typical for the ARM to adjust

The interest rate on an ARM is made up of two components, the index and the margin.

The index is a measure of interest rates and margin refers to the points added to the index rate by the lender.

The fully indexed rate is equal to the margin plus the index.

It is done to ensure a steady margin for the lender, whose own cost of funding will usually be related to the index.

Payments made by the borrower may change over time with the changing interest rate (alternatively, the term of the loan may vary). It is distinct from the graduated payment mortgage, which offers to change payment amounts but a fixed interest rate. Other forms of mortgage loan include the interest-only mortgage, the fixed-rate mortgage, the negative amortization mortgage, and the balloon payment mortgage. Adjustable rates transfer part of the interest rate risk from the lender to the borrower. They can use where variable interest rates make fixed rate loans challenging to obtain.

The borrower benefits if the interest rate falls but loses if the interest rate increases.

The borrower benefits from reduced margins to the underlying cost of borrowing compared to fixed or capped rate mortgages. A graduated payment mortgage loan often referred to as GPM, is a mortgage with low initial monthly payments which gradually increase over a specified time frame.

These plans mostly geared towards young men and women who cannot afford large payments now but can realistically expect to do better financially in the future. For instance, a medical student who is about to finish medical school might not have the financial capability to pay for a mortgage loan. Once he or she graduates, it is more than probable that they will be earning a high income.

It is a form of negative amortization loan. An interest-only loan is a loan in which, for a set term, the borrower pays only the interest on the principal balance, with the principal balance unchanged.

At the end of the interest-only term, the borrower may enter an interest-only mortgage, pay the principal, or (with some lenders) convert the loan to a principal and interest payment (or amortized) loan at his/her option.

A fixed-rate mortgage (FRM), often referred to as a "vanilla wafer" mortgage loan, is a fully amortizing mortgage loan the interest rate remains the same through the term of the loan. As opposed to loans where the interest rate may adjust or "float."

As a result, payment amounts and the duration of the loan fixed. The person who is responsible for paying back the loan. Benefits from a consistent, single payment and the stuff to plan a budget based on this fixed cost.

The most common terms are 15-years and 30-year mortgages, but shorter terms.

Amortization refers to the process of paying off debt (often from a loan or mortgage) over time through regular payments.

A portion of each payment is for interest while the remaining amount applied towards the principal balance. The percentage of interest generate versus principal in each payment.

It's determined in an amortization schedule for the term of the mortgage.

A balloon payment mortgage is a mortgage which does not fully amortize over the term of the note, thus leaving a balance due at maturity.

The final payment is called a balloon payment because of its large size. It's more common in commercial Real Estate than in residential Real Estate. A balloon payment mortgage may have a fixed or a floating interest rate. Interest rates usually expressed as a percentage of the principal for one year.

You should shop around when getting your mortgage. Be careful "shopping" your potential mortgage to too many lenders can hurt and sometimes damage your chances of getting a mortgage.

# CORPORATION

A corporation, simply as a body of persons granted a charter that legally recognizes them as a separate entity with its rights, privileges and liabilities.

A corporation is the most sophisticated and protective form of business entity.

It is a "legal person" completely separate from the individuals who own and control it.

A corporation has the power to do anything any person may do: carry on business, own property, lend and borrow money, or sue and be sued.

Most importantly, it offers its shareholder's limited liability.

Its shareholders can lose no more than their original investment; they are not liable for the debts of the corporation.

Regarding limited exposure to liability alone, it pays to incorporate to protect your assets.

If you incorporate, it's difficult for someone to attach your house, car or personal assets if your business fails or if you lose a lawsuit.

Although limited liability may be the most attractive feature of incorporating, there are many others.

For many investors, there is a great peace of mind when doing business.

When starting up a business, a business person decides if it is better to use a corporation or not.

There are many advantages to using corporations, and it is probably the most commonly used business structure. However, some disadvantages and costs should consider.

Once created, the corporation has a perpetual existence separate from the owners, directors and officers of the corporation.

When doing business in the corporation's name, most income generated can classify as corporate income.

If they said income generated under your name, it then becomes capital gains, and it will fall into a higher tax bracket.

We are not here to advise you as to liability and tax considerations of your choices for business structures. Please ensure to discuss your corporate structure with a Professional Accountant or Tax Attorney. The three most prevalent types of what are considered corporations are the C Corporation, S Corporation and LLC. The C Corporation is the most common kind of corporate entity and the one like by most large companies.

C Corporation is subject to double taxation, in that the corporation pays taxes on profits. When money is taken from the corporation as dividends by a shareholder, that money is taxable income for each shareholder.

The S Corporation structure resembles a partnership in that the profits of the corporation are passed on to the shareholder(s) as personal income; thus; there is no taxation at the corporate level.

S Corporation does protect the assets of the shareholders like any other corporation. So it is elected by many people who want to be taxed at the personal level but want to shield their assets.

LLC, Limited Liability Company, is not a corporation but a blending of the asset protection benefits of a corporation with some aspects of a partnership or sole proprietorship.

The income taxed as personal income is like proprietorship or partnership, while the protection afforded to shareholders in a Corporation also provided LCC.

# CHAPTER 4 MULTIPLE STREAM OF INCOME

One of the most devastating issues is having one stream of income, and you lost it was through a job. The loss of a job causes people sometimes to have depression, stress that can lead to alcoholism, drug addiction. To prevent those problems is to create multiple streams of Income. A large population of people as they heard multiple streams of Income; associate it with working more than one job. Multiple streams of Income go far beyond working with another job. The difference between a job and business is that a worker's execution or performance of task and business is the purchase and sale of goods in an attempt to make a profit. A job worker trade time for money, this service might pay the bills but will not make you wealthy. Your network is your net worth. Your network influenced by the people you associate with, and it determines the outcome of your net worth. The network is an association of individuals having a common interest, formed to provide mutual assistance, helpful information, or the like. Net worth is your assets. Multiple streams of Income comes from owning income properties, starting online businesses, speaking engagements. Also creating your own products, and manage your stock portfolio or a second job.

The employee got sick unable to work, and not work-related in a short period they are off the boss payroll. Apply for EI benefits that run out next stop is disability or welfare benefits.

Prosperity is available to anyone if they want it bad enough. You could be an author of a book you do the job once, but it keeps generating income for many years. Multiple streams of Income mean that you have Income from several different sources. If one source stops or eliminated, you can rely on another source. Sometimes it takes a while to establish many streams of Income. The secret the wealthy and the powerful use to built wealth is having multiple streams of income. A wealthy person, multiple streams of an income portfolio, might look something like this, income properties, stock investment, an author of a book with lots of speaking engagements.

The new trend of today society is to develop multiple streams of income if you want to survive and unmask wealth. Whether you are a low or high-income earner, you should create multiple streams of Income.

CEO of a company making a six-figure salary one day showed up at work, and told his service is no longer required. Mr. CEO was living like the Jones to keep up with societal trends living the high-end lifestyle and did not save a lot of his income and no other income stream

What will happen to him the one stream dries up? If he does not get another job fast depression, stress set in, his high-end lifestyle come to a screeching halt? Here is Joe who lost his job but was happy told the boss thanks for the opportunity to work with his company because he had multiple streams of Income.

If you only have one stream of income, you should consider having an income replacement insurance plan. If you are an employee who qualified for E.I. Benefits, the income replacement insurance starts when the E.I. runs out.

Whether you are a small or a large business, it is imperative to buy business insurance to covered employees, Loss of Income, property, e.g., in the case of fire. If you provide a full or partial income for your family, then you need to carry life insurance and disability insurance. To make sure in case of death or disability, your family financially protected. If you become sick or disabled for an extended period; have no one to take over the operation of your business, it could be in jeopardy. Disability insurance would provide at least a percentage of your income while you're not able to work.

Employee Fidelity Bonds (EFBs) it covers employee theft, embezzlement, and other fraud.

As the employer, you can purchase bonded coverage for any of your employees or buy blanket coverage for all your employees (the most common).

It prevents you from buying EFBs policy every time you hire a new employee. It is optional, but if you don't, you'll be responsible and liable for any theft or other illegal activity committed by your employee at a client's home or place of business. Sometimes it can become costly to pay out of pocket. Employee Fidelity Bonds can be purchased in various amounts, depending on the risk and type of properties you're working. If you have an employee or are thinking of hiring an employee, who has already convicted of a crime, insurance companies will not sell you an EFB for that employee. If you have the blanket coverage, they are covered.

Key people are individuals whose skills, knowledge, experience or leadership are essential to a business' continuous financial success.

If something should happen to any one of these individuals, it is likely that their loss will hurt the profitability of the business and can cause financial hardship. The key person includes company Directors, Sales Directors, IT Specialist, Managing Directors and heads of product development but is not limited to only those positions. A company purchases a life insurance policy on the key employee pays the premiums and is the beneficiary of the policy. If that person unexpectedly dies, the company receives the insurance payoff.

The categories of loss for which key person insurance can provide compensation:

1. Losses related to the extended period when a key person is unable to work, to provide temporary personnel and, and sometimes to finance the recruitment and training of a replacement.
2. Insurance to protect profits offsetting lost Income from lost sales, losses resulting from the delay or cancellation of any business project that the key person was involved in, loss of opportunity to expand, loss of specialized skills or knowledge.
3. Insurance to protect shareholders or partnership interests.
4. Insurance for anyone involved in guaranteeing business loans.

You may have a Key Person insurance cover on your life from the company you work. In case of a disability, it does not cover your personal needs, so you still need coverage separate for yourself. People do not plan to fail; they fail to plan. If you look at stream water flowing into it from many directions never dried up, it is the same paradigm with multiple streams of incomes.

# CHAPTER 5 THE KEYS TO ASSISTING RENTAL PROPERTY OWNERS SET UP AND MANAGE THEIR PROPERTIES MORE EFFECTIVELY

## COSTLY LEGAL MISTAKES THAT CAN SINK A LANDLORD BUSINESS

Being a successful Landlord requires lots of practical know-how, business sense, and familiarity with the market. The following is a list of the top ten mistakes that can sink your business.

## USING GENERIC OR OUTDATED LEASE FORMS

Most Landlords know it's essential to have a written lease or rental agreement, but using the wrong form can get you into big trouble.

So-called "standard" forms that are sold everywhere probably aren't compliant with the laws in your province or state or country. If you use a stationery store agreement that short-cuts
Tenants' rights, you could find yourself at the losing end of a lawsuit because of an unenforceable clause.
A valid lease agreement is key to assisting Rental Property Owners set up to manage their properties more efficiently.
On the other hand, some standard forms impose more significant obligations and restrictions on you than your provincial or state law does.

## ASKING THE WRONG QUESTIONS DURING APPLICANT SCREENING

Thorough Tenant screening is an essential part of your business — if you choose poorly. You're in for nothing but headaches with Tenants who don't pay the rent, trash the place, or worse. But there are limits to what you can ask.
Many Landlords don't realize that even well-meaning questions. Such as asking a disabled person about his disability or asking if a couple is married can be illegal forms of discrimination.
If the applicant doesn't get the rental, even though your rejection had nothing to do with the offending question, the disappointed Tenant now has ammunition for a fair housing complaint.

# SETTING POLICIES THAT DISCRIMINATE AGAINST FAMILIES

Even though it has been illegal to discriminate against families for over 20 years, many Landlord practices are far from family-friendly and are downright illegal.

Excluding families, because you feel children will cause more wear and tear and you prefer a "mature, quiet" environment is illegal.

And while you're permitted to limit the number of residents in a unit (in most situations, two occupants per bedroom), you may not apply that standard differently when dealing with families.

The cost of this mistake can be another trip to your lawyer's office to deal with a fair housing complaint.

# MAKING PROMISES THAT YOU DON'T DELIVER ON

Okay to be enthusiastic about the benefits of your property, it's necessary to do so in competitive markets. Understand that your enthusiastic promises will become binding if applicants rely on them when deciding to rent.

For example, you may have to deliver the goods if you assure an applicant of a parking space, satellite service, or a new paint job.

A Tenant who feels ripped off may legally break the lease or sue you for the difference in value between what was as promised and what you delivered. Whether the Tenant will win is hardly the point — you'll have to respond, which will cost time and money.

## CHARGING LATE FEES

Late fees can be a powerful tool to motivate Tenants to pay the rent on time.

## VIOLATING TENANTS' RIGHTS TO PRIVACY

Most Provinces or States have detailed rules on when, for what reasons, and with how much notice you may enter a Tenant's home. Many Landlords stop by unannounced, asking to check things over, perform an on-the-spot repair, or show the place to prospective Tenants. Repeated violations of a Tenant's privacy (or even one outrageous violation) can excuse a tenant from any further obligations under the lease and may also result in court-ordered money damages against the Landlord.
Security Deposits used in the USA
In Ontario only first and last month's rent is allowed. It is different than other Provinces in Canada.

# IGNORING DANGEROUS CONDITIONS IN AND AROUND THE DWELLING

Landlords in virtually every States or Provinces are required to offer and maintain housing that meets essential health and safety standards. Such as those set by States or Provinces and local building codes, health ordinances, and Landlord-Tenant laws.
If you fail to take care of essential repairs, deal with environmental hazards, or respond when your property. Become an easy mark for criminals; Tenants may break the lease, in many States or Provinces. Some might allow then to withhold the rent or make the repair themselves and deduct the expense from the rent.
Landlords who have failed to make their properties reasonably secure in the face of repeated on-site crime are often ordered to compensate the Tenant-victim when yet another criminal intrudes. These are expensive ways to learn the law.

# NOT FILLING OUT GOVERNMENT FORMS CORRECTLY

When a Landlord fills out an application and goes to the Landlord and Tenant Board, it is becoming commonplace for tenants to receive legal aid to assist them in finding your errors.

Failing to Understand your Position in Regards to the Law
Many rules in Ontario seem to go against "common sense" and even against the standard civil law.
Understand your position and your situation at all times.

# SOME OF THE ERRORS PROPERTY OWNERS/LANDLORDS MAKE

Being a good listener allows potential tenants to talk about themselves. It will help you with screening tenants
Do not spend time telling prospective tenants about yourself
They save no money for emergency
For renovations, not enough contingency funds are added to the budget (10-15%) to cover the unforeseen cost
They do not upgrade the rental property before renting it
They give no welcome gift
When purchasing an Income Property, make sure all units are legal.
If not, it comes back to bite you, especially if a tenant or a neighbour complains.

# TIPS FOR BEING A SUCCESSFUL LANDLORD

The key to being a successful Landlord is taking time to pick the best Tenants and keeping the rental property well maintained.

If you do not have the time to maintain the property on your own, or you own several rental properties, you can quickly become overwhelmed.

The tips provided below are the most common ways to ensure your success as a Landlord:

Get It in Writing

To protect your interests and the interests of your Tenants, get everything in writing.

It is means everything from a rental application to a code of conduct.

Tenant needs something fixed in their dwelling, ask them to provide the request in writing in addition to telling you on the phone or in person.

It will help you with your income tax deductions and create a history for each Tenant.

# PROVIDE A CLEAN & SECURE RESIDENCE

Keep the grounds of the property clean and free of debris.

It will help you with property liability and keep your rental property looking its best.

Depending on the location of the rental property, you may want to provide extra security measures. It can help keep your Tenants safe and secure, and may even lower your insurance premiums.

# PICK YOUR MANAGERS CAREFULLY

If you do not have the time to manage your rental properties personally, you will need to hire a manager. But your success as a Landlord will hinge on your choice.
Make sure to hire the absolute best person for the job.

# BE INSURED

Make sure that you have the maximum amount of rental insurance, property liability insurance, and any other type of insurance coverage required in your province/state.
It can help protect you from devastating losses.
Make Repairs Promptly
Your Tenants deserve to have decent living conditions.
In the case of furnaces and other necessary appliances and fixtures, repairs cannot be put off.
Try to imagine yourself in your renter's position.
Could you live without running water for three days?

# RESPECT THE PRIVACY OF YOUR TENANTS

Adhere to your Provinces/State's guidelines for entry into a rented dwelling.
Most Provinces/States require at least a 24-hour notice before a Tenant is required to allow their Landlord to enter their rented dwelling.

# DO NOT DISCRIMINATE

Follow the rules of the Human Rights Commission when you screen prospective Tenants.
A discrimination lawsuit is extremely costly and completely avoidable.
Give everyone an equal chance to rent your property, regardless of their race, religion, or beliefs.
Have a Well-Drafted Lease. It is imperative that the form of the lease you use with Tenants be well-drafted and Pro-Landlord-oriented as much as possible. Without anything that contradicts the Residential Tenancy Act of your Province or State.
Always Be Fair
In addition to avoiding discrimination, strive to treat all of your Tenants fairly.
Try to understand their position and keep in mind how they may perceive your actions.

While you may not be able to get along with everyone, having a good rapport with your Tenants will reduce vacancy problems.

Only you have the genuine desire to make your Landlord business succeed. Take the time to set up a proper course of action that will reduce income loss that's associated with high-risk Tenants.

# HOW TO RETAIN TENANTS AND IMPROVE YOUR BOTTOM LINE

Research shows that the majority of Tenant turnover is controllable and that Management's performance in delivering service plays the primary role in Tenant Agreement renewal decisions. With a move-out costing you $3,000-$6,000, controllable turnover cannot overlook.

Here are some tips from seasoned Property Managers on what can work to retain your Tenants. Some are very controversial, so it's up to you to decide what works best for your situation.

It's up to you to decide what works for you!

Spell out incentives in the Agreement, so Tenants have a goal to work towards.

Create Tenant incentives as a point system for timely rent payments that converts to a renewal rebate.

Keep the property in good repair. Keep the landscape trim, the outdoor lights working and the faucets from leaking means that you care.

Allow some personalization of the unit.

Communicate during the term of the lease.

Tenants often feel neglected once they've moved in. Find ways to get in front of them regularly outside of rent collection.

Give out cookies, candy and compliments. "Thanks for paying on time. I appreciate it!"

Offer an incentive each time a Tenant offers a suggestion.

Develop loyalty through seasonal parties, or seminars, like a talk on healthy eating, how to play the stock market, or how to draft a will.

Set up leagues for sports, video games, and book clubs.

Encourage them to bring friends to on-site events.

If you have a single unit, offer a restaurant certificate on a birthday or special occasion for your Tenant and a guest.

Email flyers regarding events in the neighbourhood to tenants.

Consider dedicating a sunny spot for a garden.

Let Tenants put down roots, literally, in a sunny spot. Add decorative stone and a water feature.

Place a picnic table in the backyard for barbeques.

Meditative spaces can be tiny, and low maintenance and a highly effective way of keeping your Tenants around.

Involve Tenants in community functions.

Publicize the money your Tenants collected for the local humane society, toy drive or fire department by sending a press release to the papers.

Publish a community newsletter/blog.

If you have single-family rentals, you can link your Tenant community. Find out well in advance if the Tenant is considering moving out at the end of the lease term.

Give yourself time to consider the Tenant's options and develop a counteroffer.

If you cannot change the Tenant mind, conduct an exit interview. So you can find out what would have made a difference for them. That way, you avoid having the same complaint from the next Tenant.

# WHAT DO TENANTS WANT

Nothing impacts the renewal likelihood more than how service requests handled.

The work order process begins and ends with the office, not maintenance, staff.

Work order how handled by the office and their communications with tenants. Regarding such, the strongest, relationship builder with or without retention.

Tenants might not notice a "job well done," but they certainly remember bad experiences.

Thus, the goal must be to minimize dissatisfaction, and when a bad experience occurs, to rise to the occasion and deliver a "remarkable recovery."

The top items, of what tenants want from Landlord/owner
Promptly responding to calls
Emails
Landlord/owner follows up on completed requests
Landlord/owner responsive
Dependability
Landlord/owner courteous
Professionalism
Apartment condition well maintain
Good appearance
Community safety
Quality of maintenance work
The speed of handling the request

# QUALIFY POTENTIAL NEW TENANTS

Credit Worthiness
To be a successful Landlord, you will need to determine if a prospective Tenants' credit history and payment pattern are acceptable and ensure that it meets your criteria.
To establish creditworthiness:

Some questions to ask potential tenants on the phone before setting up an appointment to show the property.
Obtain a credit report to determine payment patterns and creditworthiness
Request a W2 or Employer Pay Stub to establish an income level
Request a Bank Account Statement that shows deposits made every payday
Request a letter from Employer giving a letter of employment and salary status
Tenant Worthiness
It is different than Credit Worthiness; some tenants do not have a good credit history for various reasons. They have a good job, stable income and always pay their rent on time.
Tenant Worthiness should be a required criterion that every single prospective Tenant must meet for occupancy of your rental unit.
To establish tenant worthiness contact the current and (where applicable) previous Landlord(s) and ask these questions:
Did the prospective Tenant meet all of the terms of the lease agreement?
How many times was rent payment late?
Were there any problems with the Tenant?
What was the reason for the Tenant leaving?
Would you rent to this Individual again
Obtain a Criminal Record & Eviction Search to determine tenant worthiness further.

If a criminal record exists, what is it for? If the Tenant has previously evicted, then that is a huge red flag.

## Selecting prospective tenants

In choosing potential tenants, landlords may use, in the manner prescribed in the regulations made under the Human Rights Code, income information, credit checks, credit references, rental history.

## Questions to ask potential tenants on the phone before setting up an appointment

Before making an appointment to show the space, the owner/manager should determine the prospect's need, and precise space requirements, e.g. ask the number of bedrooms the prospect requires

Discuss whether the prospect prefers a high rise building or multitenant building

Desired price range

Parking and transportation needs

Demographic information and any amenities the tenant requires

Be honest if the initial discussion suggests that space is not suitable for that potential prospect

Rather than waste time showing the space, take the potential prospect's name and contact information

Check to see if a more appropriate unit is available if you own multiple buildings

Check urgency of needing a rental unit, e.g. Is relocation necessary or optional

When is the move planned?

Why are they moving?

Is this a temporary location or a long-term move?

Check whether the prospect is the decision-maker or someone else

# PREPARING AND SHOWING THE PROPERTY

If another tenant is living in the apartment, remind them between the hours of 9-5 p.m. the unit will show to potential tenants.

Encourage present tenants to keep the unit clean for showing.

Check the unit about 10 -15 minutes before showing it to ensure it is in excellent condition.

Do not show the vacant unit to more than one tenant at a time. It can cause chaos.

Some landlords feel showing a vacant unit to more than one tenant at a time will put pressure on the prospective tenants to make a decision.

It has a more negative impact because prospective tenants will not feel respected and will internalize it. Feel if they rent that unit they would not treat with respect and dignity.

Schedule the vacant unit showing by about 30-45 minutes apart. That allows the landlord to have time to answer potential tenant questions and complete application.

Remember the first impression you give a prospective tenant will be a lasting one.

To attract the best quality tenants, you need to make sure that your property is in excellent condition.

Preparing your income property goes a long way to ensuring that your property stays tenanted.

Ideally, you will want to be able to select the best possible tenant from a good pool of applicants.

The better the condition the building in the more options you will have.

Good quality tenants do not want to stay in buildings which are run down and unclean.

Your investment in the property will offset by the fact that your tenants stay longer. Has a lower level of turnover, and less damage is caused through neglect by your tenants.

# CLOSING TECHNIQUES TO USE WITH PROSPECTIVE TENANTS

The manager may want to repeatedly summarize the benefits throughout the showing to show the indecisive prospect that space is ideal

The manager may ask direct questions aimed at eliciting an affirmative decision, e.g. "which space do you prefer."

Emphasizes the fact that space satisfies the potential tenant's needs

Prepare Applications for new tenants

Show Property Owners/Landlords how to prepare applications and have all lease agreements signed.

Prepare Landlord/Tenants Inspection Check List for new tenants and take pictures of the rental units.
Prepare Welcome Letters for new tenants.
A free copy of Information for New Tenants from the Landlord and Tenant Board in Ontario should give to new tenants.
Place all of the applications in a file folder for the new tenants
Record Keeping
Keep track of everything using the software necessary (e.g. Outlook, Excel, or any database management software).
Keep all client and customer records under tight security.
Get consent from clients and customers before distributing any personal information.
The Personal Information Protection and Electronic Documents Act (PIPEDA or the PIPED Act) is a Canadian law relating to data privacy. It governs how private sector organizations collect, use and disclose personal information in the course of commercial business.
Document all communication.
Be clear and concise.
Invest in a good printer with scanner and fax features.
Lots of business owners invest in a business in a box or a filing cabinet full of folders that they tend to misplace information.

Waste a lot of valuable time going through the box or filing cabinet to find a small piece of paper, especially during income tax time.

Let's manage your time and business more effectively by creating folder/folders on your computer and scan the documents e.g. receipts, tenant's application.

The risk of you misplacing another document is low when on the computer.

So what if the computer crashes? No problem always back up your documents on a USB stick or online via Google or Yahoo for a monthly fee.

How to make an excel spreadsheet do your basic accounting for monthly expenses.

It does not replace your accountant but reduces your cost of accounting fees.

Keeping accurate records is essential to the proper running of your property.

If you run into any problems with your tenants, you will need to have accurate records to back up your claims.

The courts will require less of the tenants than they do of the landlord as it assumed you are running your property in a business-like manner.

It is most helpful when having multiple rental properties.

# MAXIMIZE YOUR CASH FLOW

Improve property by painting, landscaping and doing minor repairs.

Add coin laundry in the building of three or more units. Chargeless for washing and more for drying.

Consider adding basic cable to the building of each unit (charge about $30-40.00 per month).

Add wireless internet in building for all units (charge about $35-40.00 per month).

Charge for parking if possible in your area (charge $25-50 per month)

Re-organize units to create more usage. Convert two-bedroom apartments to a possible three room's rental.

Recommended charges for extra storage space $50.00-$100.00 per month.

Install energy savers light bulb.

Convert the garage into personal storage for each unit.

Install tankless water heater and save 25% monthly on utility bills (works best in buildings where Property Owner pay all the utilities.

Change all standard fuses to breaker fuses (breaker fuses effortlessly to press reset)

Install a digital programmable thermostat. Allows you to control the temperature for the season and has a security password.

You can make up to four settings each day with the help of a digital thermostat. Digital thermostats widely acclaimed for its high precision and flexibility.
Rent your Property in short a period (15 days or less) and Minimize Vacancy Rate
How you present your rental unit is key to prospective Tenants.
Ensure the unit shown with great light.
Ensure the landscape well kept.
In wintertime shovel snow and salt area for safety
Use neutral colours when painting units
Have unit clean and smelling fresh
Fix broken window and door screens
Store toys in one location
Ensure appliances clean before showing unit
Paint walls with a high gloss finish (save from painting walls frequently. Wash walls instead)
Keep countertops clean and clear
Replace old silicon from bathroom tubs
Fix leaky faucet to prevent brown stains
Paint small rooms with lighter colours to make them seem bigger
Tighten all loose handles on doors and cabinets
Uncluttered the unit if it is possible
Present the inside and outside of your property to make the first impression.

# HOW TO HAVE A CONTINGENCY FUND FOR EMERGENCY

Some Property Owners do not plan for an emergency, e.g. plumbing problem, broken appliances. Remember as the property owner's your goal is to ensure the tenants get proper service at all time You should have a start out contingency fund of $500- $1000 minimum, then keep adding to it $50-100 per month.  Have about three months mortgage in your account if possible in case of disaster, e.g. fire, flood . and have no tenants while repairs get done to the property.

# RESPECTING YOUR TENANTS

The first rule is to ensure your tenants have a well-kept environment in which to live no matter what the situation
Prompt to follow- up and do the necessary repairs to their units
Effective communication with tenants related to their issues or concerns
Keep in mind that without tenants you would not have an income property
Treat all tenants fairly and with the same respect. e.g. Allowing John to change his car oil in the driveway but Tom cannot

# ADVERTISING A PROPERTY

Where to promote your ad for your vacant apartment/house.
To get the best results and rent in a shorter time frame place your advertisement on KIJIJI.ca, Craigslist.org, and View it.ca.
When writing an ad listing, the major intersection and great selling features, e.g. recently renovated; the size of the apartment, 1or2 bedrooms, balcony, close to TTC, shopping centre, parks, no pets, no smoking, laundry facility, if it has an extra unsuited bathroom. Also, put your contact person name and phone number.
Do not put an address on the ad because people will show up anytime without calling to see the apartment.

# SOME OTHER ADVERTISING METHODS FOR REACHING A TARGET AUDIENCE

Newspapers
Internet
Brochures
Flyers
Advertise by word of mouth, ask present tenants
Video on YouTube

Newspaper advertising divided into two types: classified and display ads.

Classified ads are relatively reasonably priced per line of copy and are the most predominant method of residential advertising properties.

Display ads, on the other hand, carry more significant visual impact than the classifieds because they are larger and more sophisticated in designs.

Display ads also cost more. It is excellent to keep accurate records of the number of prospects generated by advertising, to judge the effectiveness.

Jane Way Dr: Large art deco one bedroom newly renovated $775. Immediate occupancy Call John 416 477-9494

This ad is great for a low vacancy rate area, but if it were a high vacancy rate area, it would not be as highly effective.

In a high vacancy rate area, the ad would require better selling features, e.g. if it has a balcony, close to the local transit system, shopping center.

Jane Way Dr: Newly renovated Luxury 1 bedroom penthouse Apt with den $900. Rooftop sundeck and fitness centre. Video controlled entry

This ad would be more effective in a high vacancy rate area to reach your target market because it highlights some of the great features of the apartment. Example owner has an apartment renting for $1,100 in a high vacancy rate area.

Takes out a $75 per day classified ad, for five consecutive days to find a tenant.

The total cost is $375, which the property owner might think quite high.

The expense is justifiable because it results in a one year lease worth $13,200 ($1,100x12)

The owner takes out a $75 once per week classified ad for five weeks to find a tenant for the same property.

The total cost is still $375 for advertising cost, but the owner lost $1,100 for a month.

Under the circumstances, finding the new tenant will cost about $1475 (1,100+375)

The owner reduced the rent to $100 to attract prospects, with a $75 one day advertisement on the internet.

The total cost is $75 for advertising, but the owner lost $1,200 over a one year lease period to find a tenant. ($100x12) The total cost to find a tenant $1275 (1,200+75)

# WRITING A FAIR RENTAL HOUSING AD

Landlords and tenants want to comply with housing-related laws, but they don't always know all the rules. Both landlord and tenant groups want to increase awareness about human rights in housing and to end discrimination.

The Ontario Human Rights Commission created this guide to help landlords who are advertising their rental units. Organizations that provide housing listings to prevent human rights violations and avoid complaints.

What Ontario's Human Rights Code Says?

You cannot deny a tenant housing because of:

Receipts of public assistance, like welfare or employment insurance

Race, colour or ethnic origin

Age, including 16- or 17-year-olds who are independent of their parents

Family status

Marital status, including people with common-law or same-sex partners

Ancestry, including people of Aboriginal descent

Sex, including pregnancy and gender identity

Religious beliefs or practices

Place of origin

Sexual orientation

Disability

Citizenship, including refugee status.

People also protected from discrimination for being a friend or relative of someone identified by one of the above grounds.

Writing a fair rental housing AD

These rules do not apply where a tenant shares a bathroom or kitchen with the landlord or the landlord's family.

Some housing ads contain statements that openly discriminate:

"Adult building" or "Not suitable for children."

"Must have working income" or "Must provide proof of employment."

"No ODSP"

"Seeking mature couple."

These ads discriminate because they show the landlord's preference of some people over others. Based on Human Rights Code grounds like marital or family status, age, disability and receipt of public assistance (including if a person's income is from student loans, the Ontario Disability Support Program or Ontario Works, pension or retirement funds).

## SOME ADS DISCRIMINATE BY ACCIDENT

Some landlord when listing "selling points" to attract tenants, make statements that may discriminate. Even if they don't mean to; it often happens when you are trying to appeal to people you think may like the rental unit.

Some examples are:

Ideal for a quiet couple

Suitable for single professional

Perfect for female student

Suits mature individual or couple

Great for working folks or students.

These statements suggest that the landlord prefers some people over others based on the Code grounds listed above. These ads discourage good tenants from applying because they think they won't treat fairly.

Other common statements that might discriminate are:

Not soundproof" – may indicate bias against families with children

"No pets" – Under Ontario's Human Rights Code, persons with disabilities who use service animals (such as guide dogs) cannot be denied access to any housing based on a "no pets" rule

# COLLECTING RENTAL INCOME

Use of Credit Card online with PayPal on the website

Wireless machine for large rental properties

Post-dated Cheques

Cash or Money Order

Authorized debit

Online through PayPal- free to set up, accept Visa, Master Card and American Express

# OPERATING COSTS

Salaries.

Cost of Utilities not charged to the tenants pay by the owner.
Contract services such as lawn maintenance, elevator maintenance, rubbish removal.
Supplies and equipment.
Advertising and management.

# PROPERTY SAFETY

Smoke detector in each unit (might reduce property insurance).
Consider installing interconnected smoke alarms on every level of the property, have it hardwired to your house power system.
Carbon Monoxide detector in various parts of the building and each unit.
Fire extinguisher in every kitchen.
A Dead-bolt lock on the main entrance and every unit door.
Keep property clear of any debris.
Look for loose and hanging electrical wires.
Install alarm system (don't pay for the installation, only the monitoring)
Control Rehabilitation and Maintenance Expense
Inspect and improve property every 3-4 months
Clean unit before new tenants moves in
Fix all leaky pipes and faucets

Hire a tenant to do minor repairs, take out the garbage and clean the property (maximum $50-$100.00 per month).

# UPGRADES

The decision whether or not to upgrade your property will depend in large part on the effect it will have on your rental return.

Before making any upgrade, it is essential to determine whether you will see this returned in excess rental income.

We use the payback period of the upgrade to determine whether or not it is a good idea and if we want to go ahead.

The formula for the payback period is as follows:

Payback period = Cost of upgrade / Increase in a monthly increase

For example, if you have decided to install a stove in the apartment unit, which you will calculate will cost approximately $200.

And your analysis shows that apartments with new stoves rent for about $10 more a month.

Then the payback period would be calculated as follows: 20 Months = 200 / 10

Whether or not you wish to proceed with the improvement is whether you consider this an acceptable timeframe or not to be paid back for your investment.

Important to remember when you make upgrades to the property, you are also increasing the overall capital value of the property as well.

The capital value of the property is the inverse of the rental yield as well as the fact that properties that well maintained fetch a higher price.

The primary determining factor though, should be the time the investment takes to pay back.

# FINDING A CONTRACTOR

Get a referral from friends, family and neighbours.
Ask Contractors for references from previous clients.
Ask Contractors for their business license number and check with the licensing office and their insurance company for public liability and property damage insurance.
Get at least three estimates before starting the work
Have a complete description of work to be done
What type of work do you specialize in
The contract should contain the client's name, address (if different from the worksite) and complete address of the property where the work will get done.
Contractor's information should request name, address, telephone and registered business numbers.
Start and completion dates.

Termination clause- gives the client the option to terminate the contract.

The price and payment schedule.

Agreement on who is responsible for all necessary permits, licenses and inspections.

Contractor's responsibilities include public liability insurance, property damage insurance and removal of construction debris when the job finished

Use more sub-contractors instead of employees

After a contractor is finishing the job, he/she might ask you to sign a completion certificate, inspect the work first before the sign.

If the contractor has to come back to complete minor details could to weather condition, you make a note of it. Possibly hold back a percentage of the payment to cover the remaining work.

Some contractor offers a warranty on their work if something goes wrong in a particular period they will fix it. Do not pay the contractor all the payment upfront give a certain percentage as the work progress as included in your contract. Upon completion, if still need to do the minor job, you can use the holdback clause.

# THERE ARE THREE TYPES OF HOLDBACKS

Deficiency holdback – a project is considered complete, often some deficient items and that might need to be corrected.

Seasonal holdback – depending on the time of year that the project developed, might be items that cannot complete.

Builders lien holdback – it proposed to provide homeowners with protection should subcontractors or suppliers place liens against the property. To secure payment for work performed and might not pay by the general contractor for their services rendered.

A team of Personnel Required to Service or to do Maintenance on your property

Handyman 2

Plumber 2

Landscaper 2

Electrician 2

Pest Control Company 2

Small Appliance Repair Person 2

Stager 2

Cleaning Company 2

Tax Accountant

Mortgage Broker

Personal Banker

A Lawyer or Legal Assistance

# 3 DIFFERENT TYPES OF COMMERCIAL REAL ESTATE LEASES

Three Basic Types of Leases
Gross Lease
Net lease
Percentage lease

Gross lease: The most frequently used tenancy agreement is in the form of a gross lease, whereby the Tenant pays a fixed rent. The owner covers all of the expenses which associated with the operation of the property including Taxes, Insurance, Utilities Other expenses. Extraordinary repairs may negotiate between the parties.

Net lease: the second type of lease, under which the tenant not only pays the rent but in addition to this, also assumes responsibility for certain expenses associated with the leased premises. The landlord then receives a net figure as rent. Within this type of lease, there are three sub-types of net leases (Single-net lease, Net-net lease, Net-net-net lease).

Single-net lease: Under the Single-net lease, the tenant pays for maintenance and operating expenses associated with the space leased.

Net-net lease: Under the Net-net lease, the tenant pays all the maintenance and operating expenses, plus the property taxes.

Net-net-net lease: Under the Net-net-net lease (also known as the triple–net lease) the tenant pays all maintenance and operating expenses, property taxes and the insurance. The net lease and its variations are usually long-term leases that have designed for commercial properties such as large office building. The advantage of a Percentage lease from the tenant's point of view is that it is a long-term lease with a minimum fair rental. It is obligating the tenant to pay additional amounts only when business volume justifies an increase. The owner is allowed to share in the increasing value of business volume and the location.

# PRIVACY AND ACCESS

A landlord can enter a tenant's rental unit without written notice if there is an emergency such as a fire. The tenant agrees to let the landlord in; a care home tenant has agreed in writing that the landlord can come in to check on their condition at regular intervals.

A landlord can enter a rental unit without written notice, between 8 a.m. and 8 p.m. if the rental agreement requires the landlord to clean the unit – unless the agreement allows different hours for cleaning.

The landlord or tenant has given a notice of termination, or they have an agreement to end the tenancy. The landlord wants to show the unit to a potential new tenant (in this case, although notice is not required, the landlord must try to tell the tenant before entering for this reason).

Entry with 24 hours written notice

A landlord can enter the rental unit between 8 a.m. and 8 p.m., and only if they have given the tenant 24 hours written notice:

To make repairs or do work in the unit.

To carry out an inspection, where reasonable, to determine whether repairs are needed,

To allow a potential mortgagee or insurer of the complex to view the unit,

To enable a prospective purchaser to see the rental unit. Note: the Act also allows a registered Real Estate Agent or Broker to enter for this purpose if they have written authorization from the landlord),

To let an Engineer, Architect or another similar professional to make an inspection or for any reasonable purpose authorized by the rental agreement.

The notice must include the reason why the landlord wants to enter the rental unit and must state what time, between 8 a.m. and 8 p.m., the landlord will enter the unit.

If the landlord gives the tenant the correct notice, the landlord can enter even if the tenant is not at home.

# NOTICE OF TERMINATION

A notice of termination from either a landlord or a tenant must:

Be in writing

Identify the dwelling

Specify the date the rental unit is to vacate (the termination date)

Be signed by the person giving the notice

A notice of termination from a landlord must also:

State the reason and supporting details for termination of tenancy

Show that a tenant is not forced to leave just because the notice served. The landlord may apply to the court to regain possession of the unit

A tenant has the right to dispute the application

Serve a Notice of Termination:

For Monthly Tenancies- at least 60 days before the last day of the final month of the tenancy.

For Fixed Term Tenancies- at least 60 days before the last day of the tenancy.

For Weekly Tenancies- at least 28 days before the last day of the final week of the tenancy.

Early Termination by a Landlord: The Act allows a landlord to give a tenant notice. If the tenant, the tenant's guest or someone else who lives in the rental unit either does something. They should not do or does not do something they should.

***For example***:

Failure to pay the rent in full,

Persistently paying the rent late,

Causing damage to the rental property,

Illegal activity,

Affecting the safety of others,

Disturbing the enjoyment of other tenants or the landlord,

Allowing too many people to live in the rental unit ("overcrowding"),

Not reporting income in subsidized housing.

In some cases, a landlord can give a tenant notice based on the presence or conduct of a pet the tenant is keeping, such as where a pet causes damage to the rental property.

# TENANTS INSURANCE

As a standard practice, the property owner should notify, in writing, all tenants that they must obtain renter's insurance to protect their personal belongings.

It helps to explain insurable interest; a landlord cannot buy coverage if he or she does not own their personal belongings.

# PROPERTY OWNER INSURANCE

Have readily available the names of the insurance company for each property and the policy numbers of the policies that cover the managed properties. Know the phone number of the agent that handles the policies

Have the contact information for the claim department of the insurance company

A property owner moved out of their home, converting the home to a rental property, and insurance policy must be changed to reflect rental units.

All mortgage companies will offer you mortgage life insurance at an additional monthly cost.

It would pay off the balance of the mortgage if you were to die.

It might seem like excellent security, and it can be for you and your family, in most cases, it does not worth the cost.

For example, the balance on your mortgage was $300,000 you buy the mortgage insurance for that amount; you die owing only $50,000 the insurance company pay off the current balance.

Insurance payments remain the same throughout the payment of the mortgage even though the amount of the mortgage kept reducing.

For a higher premium, you can get conventional life insurance to cover the mortgage and have a higher payout value. Let's use the same above example you by a conventional policy for $300,000 equal value of the mortgage.

Upon your death owe $50,000 your family get $250,000 from the life insurance and $50,000 going to pay off the bank holding the mortgage.

Insurance premium can be higher for a rental property.

The insurance income property owner should obtain rental property insurance. It covers loss of rent in case there is unforeseen damage to the property and tenants have to move out for repairs to get done.

Liability insurance is vital in case of a lawsuit.

A disaster strikes such as a fire or a flood then you will need to claim with your insurance company.

When you make your claim, you will need to submit what is called a statement of loss.

It will list the items that are damaged or missing as a result of the disaster.

It is essential that you have an inventory of what is on your property and proof to back up your claim.

If you have made any purchases retain the receipts and for larger items, it is a good idea to photograph them as well.

The more proof you can provide the faster your claim can settle and the less likely it is to be disputed.

# HOW TO FIND AN INSURANCE AGENT

Arrange a meeting with at least three Insurance Agents

Have a list of properties you are interested in to purchase. Inform them usage of the property will use for income property.  Whether you live in part and rent out the other areas or if it will be a full income property.

Have all the Agents quote you umbrella policy that includes all your insurance needs. Keep in mind that having all your insurance with one company has an advantage.

Ask if you have deadbolt locks on doors, a smoke detector that is interconnected. So it goes off in one unit it rings in the others too, security monitoring system. What kind of discount will you receive on your policy?

What is the advantage of remaining with the Insurance Company for a more extended period is there some benefit to you as the client, e.g. reduction in premium.

Then compare the prices and quality of customer service and how comfortable you felt with the person.

# LAWYER

There are two types of Real Estate Lawyers those that handle lawsuits called litigators and the other who handle contract matters called transactional Lawyers.
Any Lawyer who cannot give you a half-hour free initial consultation is not worth seeing

# KNOW THE TENANCY LAWS IN YOUR AREA

Many Landlords end up paying thousands of dollars in Landlord and Tenant Board and court awards.
They make the BIG mistake of not having familiarized themselves with local tenancy laws.
It usually happens when the Tenant takes legal action against a Landlord who is unaware of his/her responsibilities.
Landlords should be aware that there are tenants who target Landlords who don't know the law.
It is incumbent upon every Landlord to know the tenancy laws so that liability and risk are minimized and completely prevented.
There is no excuse for not knowing your Provincial tenancy laws.

# HOW TO RESOLVE TENANT DISPUTES

A successful Landlord will prepare for disputes that will inevitably arise with new Tenants.

Being prepared will help you avoid being caught unaware in a stressful dispute.

Instead of immediately going to the Landlord and Tenant Board, there are many other options for resolving property disputes.

You can even state in your rental agreement what steps you will take to remedy a dispute.

Avoid Disputes by Knowing the Law

The best way to resolve disputes is by avoiding them before they even begin.

Many problems arise because one party does not know they have broken the agreement or they are not aware of their rights under the law.

Taking the time to learn the law will help you avoid disputes and make you a successful Landlord.

Keep Your Cool When a situation arises, never lose your temper, even if your Tenant does.

Be calm as possible and always do your best to take care of the situation on your own.

If you are having difficulty, or if your Tenant is not cooperating, you may need to seek assistance in court. However, by keeping your cool, you are representing yourself in the best possible light, and there is less chance the situation will escalate.

Talk It Out

Many problems with Tenants can resolve if the issue is discussed thoroughly on both sides.

Do not let your temper flare, even if you are justifiably angry.

There may be a simple answer to a problem, and both of you may be blowing it out of proportion. Working it out between two parties is almost always cheaper and more comfortable in the long term. Meet Face to Face You have traded angry words over the phone with your Tenant; a face-to-face meeting may help. Hold the meeting in a neutral territory where both of you will feel safe.

Get a Professional Mediator  If you have tried without success to resolve the dispute, a professional mediator may be able to assist you.

Many Provinces now provide property-dispute mediators who are trained to deal with situations that can arise with rental properties. Submit to Arbitration at the Landlord and Tenant Board Arbitration is similar to mediation, but arbitration is binding.

An Adjudicator will hear both sides of the case and issue a binding ruling to which you must adhere. If you are worried you are in the wrong; you probably won't want to take this step.

Instead, own up to the problem and try to settle with your Tenant.

Document Everything

A paper trail is your best defence.

A tenant has repeatedly broken the rules of your Tenancy Agreement. If they have made unreasonable demands, thorough documentation can help prove your case.

Keep a file on each Tenant and record all that transpires.

Presenting this documentation to your Tenant may even dissuade them from taking you to court. Let the Legal Reps decide .

Many cases can resolve through an agreement to settle which negotiate through lawyers or paralegals at the Landlord and Tenant Board.

If you and your Tenant are both represented by a legal rep, they may help settle the case out of court.

Small Claims Court

When a tenant moves out, you can file against them in Small Claims Court.

Be careful, because tenants who have moved out have a year to make a claim against you at the Landlord and Tenant Board!

Proceeding with Litigation

If you have exhausted all other avenues, you may have to take your case to civil or criminal court.

The actions of your Tenant will dictate your decision. Make sure that your lawyer is well versed in Residential Tenancy law and capable of prosecuting the case successfully.

Taking the time to work through a problem with a Tenant may save you time, money, and effort. Remember, the Landlord and Tenant Board is the proper avenue if the Tenant is still living in your unit.

# HOW TO PREVENT MOLD

Molds are biological pollutants that require a cellulosic food source and moisture to grow.
Molds can grow on almost any surface behind wallpaper, underneath bathtubs and flooring, an air conditioning system, and drywall.
Keep the area dry and spray with a non-toxic mold control solution.
Mold inhibitors can be added to paints to discourage mold growth further.

# VACANCY RATE

Research vacancy rates online for your neighbourhood
When renting out an income property, you want to ensure that you are charging market rent.
Check the cost of rents for similar properties in your local neighbourhood as a guide to what you should be charging.

Act like a tenant if you were searching for an apartment. Look in your community newspapers at comparable rentals to get general information about the market.

## TYPE OF NEIGHBORHOOD

Neighbourhood ideals can differ in price by being on opposite sides of an intersection or street.
You have to determine if you should remove a bathtub and have the only shower or putting a dishwasher or not, base on the clientele you are trying to attract and the neighbourhood.

## PETS

Pets can take a toll on your property, so make sure to ask about dogs or cats. Make sure you know the rules to rent an apartment with pets.

## MAXIMUM NUMBER OF TENANTS

You don't want to rent if it is going to be occupied by more than two people per bedroom.
The only real exception to this is if it is a couple with an infant child.

The more people that are on a property, the more worn it will become.
A large group of people in a small space will also generate a lot of noise which can drive out other tenants.

# LEASE AGREEMENT

Tenancy agreement means a written, oral or implied agreement between a tenant and a landlord for occupancy of a rental unit and includes a licence to occupy a rental unit.

"Tenant" includes a person who pays rent in return for the right to occupy a rental unit and consists of the tenant's heirs, assigns and personal representatives. But "tenant" does not include a person who has the right to occupy a rental unit by being. A lease is a binding contract, and both landlord and the tenant need to get everything you have agreed in writing.

Ask your lawyer to review your Lease Agreement
The landlord and tenant can sign a written agreement when a new tenancy enters into, or they can have an oral agreement.

A tenancy agreement is often called a lease. The landlord must give the tenant a copy of any written lease. The lease should not contain any terms that are inconsistent with the Act.

If the lease does include a term that is inconsistent with the Act, that term will not enforce by the Board. The landlord must also give the tenant the landlord's legal name and address so that the tenant can give the landlord any necessary notices or documents. Whether there is a written or oral lease, landlords must provide new tenants with information about the rights and responsibilities of landlords and tenants and the role of the Landlord and Tenant Board.

Landlords must give information to a tenant on or before the start of the tenancy, form approved by the Board. The Board has a two-page brochure that landlords should use for this purpose in Ontario. When a new tenancy entered into, the landlord and tenant decide how much the rent will be for a rental unit. Which services will include in the rent, for example, parking, cable, heat, electricity?

A good lease is your protection against a lawsuit. It could protect you if you hauled into court.

Your provincial/state law - and even city and town bylaws - may dictate specific policies, rents and other significant factors.

Make sure you are using a lease template that is specific to your province/state and local laws. For example, in Ontario, a "no pets" clause in the lease isn't legal because a guard dog cannot refuse. If in doubt, have an attorney look over your final draft. It's worth it!

Some landlords recommend you don't give a long-term lease.

If you are renting to someone for the first time, start with a short or month to month tenancy.

If things go badly, you will have an easier time to get them out of your property.

As the landlord, you can set up a rental agreement for any time frame you like.

Typically, leases are for one year, but you can write a 6-month lease, a 9-month

Lease – whatever you prefer.

If you do not want to commit to a year, you can offer a month-to-month rental agreement.

This type of agreement is as legally binding as a lease, but either party can get out of the contract more effectively. Some landlords prefer the flexibility of renting month-to-month, pointing out that if tenants want out of a yearlong lease. They are likely to break it anyway with no repercussions—except the landlord's rushed scramble to find new tenants.

Also, depending on where you are a month-to-month agreement can give you more opportunity to increase rents, as opposed to a lease that will lock you into a monthly amount.

Others prefer the security of a yearlong lease, which is more conducive to long-term tenants.

It translated into less time and effort spent on advertising and showing the property and screening and choosing tenants.

Getting a tenant to sign your required legal documents can be a challenging task after he/she has the keys and is in possession of the rental property.

Even if the renter fails to sign the rental contract, an oral landlord-tenant relationship established when you give him or her the keys to the unit, when you're relying on verbal agreements, you and the tenant are likely to disagree on the terms.

Regaining possession of your rental unit can be a long and expensive process, so be sure that every adult occupant signs all documents before handing over the keys.

# WHAT A RENTAL AGREEMENT INCLUDES

Regardless of which type of rental agreement you decide to use, there are specific features you must include in your legal protection.

Full legal names of the landlord(s) and tenant(s). If other occupants besides the lease signers are accepted, name them as well.

# THE STARTING DATE OF THE TENANCY

If you are allowing someone to move in ahead of time, don't change the commencement date.
Pro-Rate the rent for any early occupancy and provide a receipt to the tenant.
Indicate how much the monthly rent is, and when it is due.
Keep things consistent. Make rent due on the 1st and not the 15th or any other strange combination of due dates.
What is the term of the lease?
When does it start, when does it end?

# UTILITIES

Specify who is responsible for every utility.
If new tenants are going to be responsible for heat and hydro, put it in writing.
If they don't have their accounts in place as required, you are not obliged to release the key to them.
Landlord's Address for Service
It can be your home address, your legal representative's address, even a post office box.
In some provinces (such as Ontario) without this information, your tenant is not obliged to pay rent, so don't leave it out!

How to rent will be delivered to the landlord each month. Your tenants are responsible for getting the rent to you, not the other way around! If you don't get this information straight in your lease, you could very well be chasing your tenant for rent each month, on their terms.

Instead, consider some of these options: direct deposit into your separate rental account, email money transfer, Pay Pal, regular mail.

Appliances and other services

If you include appliances, put them in the lease.

## SPECIAL CLAUSES

It is the part of the lease that covers things such as the two cats you agreed to, the parking instructions, the smoking policy for the property. How you expect to inform of any maintenance issues, your agreement as to lawn care and snow removal, garbage, insurance.

## WHAT ELSE SHOULD I DO WHEN SIGNING THE LEASE

You have your future tenants in front of you. Both sides have gone through the lease. Now it's the time also to get some other essential things worked out and signed!

Incoming Inspection Report

If the unit is freshly painted and renovated and free of maintenance defects, get it in writing.

Have your new tenant sign off on this Report, which should include a set of photos depicting the state of the unit and appliances you include.

Smoke Alarm Maintenance Report

You've heard the horror stories: tenant rips down alarm, the house catches fire, landlord fined and charged! Start a paper trail by getting the tenant to sign off on everything in the lease.

Maintenance and Repair Request

Make sure you have a set-out way for tenants to contact you for non-emergency repair requests. Otherwise, you could have your dinners and late-night movie watching interrupted with phone calls over a dripping faucet.

Before your tenant signs, the rental contract carefully and methodically reviews each clause. Specific clauses in the rental contract are so vital that you should have the tenant specifically initial them to indicate he's read these points. They understand his or her rights and responsibilities related to the specific clauses.

For example, the tenant should initial the clause concerning the need for him or her to obtain his own renter's insurance policy. To protect his property and cover him from potential liability claims.

Have your new tenant initial that he's received the keys for the rental property and acknowledged that you had the locks rekeyed or changed since the last tenant vacated.

It's always nice to have a third party witness your lease signing (in case things go south later on).

# RENEWING A LEASE

The end of a lease does not mean a tenant has to move out. A new lease can make, or the landlord and tenant can agree to renew the lease for another fixed term period. If a new agreement not reached, the tenant still has the right to stay:

As a monthly tenant, if they paid their rent by the month in the expired lease, or

As a weekly tenant, if they paid their rent by the week in the expired lease.

Where the tenant stays on as a monthly or weekly tenant, all the rules of the former lease will still apply to the landlord and tenant.

But the landlord can increase the rent each year by the amount allowed under the Act.

# IF A TENANT WANTS TO LEAVE

A tenant must give their landlord written notice if they plan to move out.

The proper form for this notice (Form N9) is available from the Board.

A tenant and landlord can agree to end a tenancy early.

The parties can make an oral agreement to end the tenancy, but it is best to have a written agreement.

Notice of termination need not given by either the landlord or the tenant if there is an agreement to end the tenancy.

# TENANCY AGREEMENTS

The landlord must deliver a copy of the agreement to the tenant within 21 days after the tenant has signed it.

If the landlord does not meet the 21 days deadline, the tenant does not have to keep any of the promises set out in the tenancy agreement until a copy of it delivered.

As long as a landlord holds a security deposit, he/she must pay the tenant interest annually at the rate of 3-6% of the amount.

A landlord cannot require a tenant to provide post-dated cheques for rent

# MOVE-IN

You will need to organize a date which is acceptable to move in.

If you have already discussed a date you should at this point confirm that this is the day that they want to move in.

Seldom either you or the tenant will want to change the agreed-upon date.

After the existing tenants move out, you may find that the unit had hidden problems or was in worse condition than you thought.

In this case, you may need more time to fix the problems before the tenant can move in.

If this is the case, you will need to communicate with the tenant and explain why they will not be able to move in immediately.

# ENDING A TENANCY

When a fixed-term tenancy agreement expires without the landlord and tenant entering into a new agreement. The tenancy is automatically renewed on a month to month basis under the same terms and conditions as the expired agreement.

Move out procedure

Visit the rental unit a few weeks before the tenants leave to see the condition of the unit.

Offer tenant $50.00 or $100.00 incentives to keep the unit clean for showing and clean up after they move out. Inspect the rental unit the day before the tenant moves out.

# GOVERNMENT RENT SUBSIDY PROGRAMS

The government has subsidized programs that are available for tenants who are having trouble making the rent payments.
Situations sometimes unavoidable, tenants lose their jobs.
Always try to help your tenants, so they are aware you value them, especially if we're renting from you a long time.
The Rent Bank Program provides limited, interest-free loans and to seniors, individuals, and families who face eviction for rental arrears.
The maximum loan available to a household can be up to two months' rent.
The Rent Bank Program also provides emergency rental deposit loans to people affected by the recession.  Who require first and last month's rent to move to more affordable housing.
www.Rentbank.com

# RENT

"Rent" includes the amount of any consideration paid given required to be paid, presented by or on behalf of a tenant to a landlord. Landlord's agent the right to occupy a rental unit and for any services and facilities and any privilege, accommodation or thing that the landlord provides for the tenant in respect of the occupancy of the rental unit. Whether or not a separate charge made for services and facilities or the privilege, accommodation or thing, but "rent" does not include.

"Rental unit" means any living accommodation used or intended for use as rented residential premises, and "rental unit" includes.

In most cases, the rent cannot increase until at least 12 months after the tenant moved in.

The rent deposit can only use as the rent payment for the last month or week before the tenant moves out. It cannot apply to anything else, such as repairing damage to the rental unit.

If the landlord gives the tenant a notice to increase the rent, the landlord can also ask the tenant to raise the rent deposit by the same amount.

A landlord must pay the tenant interest on the rent deposit every year. Under the Act, the interest rate is the same as the rent increase guideline

When a landlord and a new tenant agree to enter into a rental agreement, they usually discuss how the rent paid.

Although the landlord and tenant can agree that the rent paid by post-dated cheques or automatic payments such as debits from a tenant's account or by credit card, a landlord cannot require the tenant to pay by either of those methods.

Once the landlord and tenant have agreed on a method of payment, it cannot change unless both the landlord and tenant agree.

Setting the rent for your property is one of the essential tasks that you will do when managing the property.

If the rent for the property is set too high, then you will probably have difficulty renting the property.

The time that lost due to the property being untenanted must also take into consideration.

Of course, if the rent is too low, then owning the unit becomes uneconomic.

You want to make sure that the rental income at a minimum covers your costs and preferably provides you with excess profit on your investment.

# RENT RECEIPTS

A landlord must give the tenant a receipt for any rent payment, rent deposit or another charge if the tenant asks for one.

A landlord must also give a former tenant a receipt if that person asks for one within 12 months after the end of their tenancy.

The landlord cannot charge a fee for giving a receipt.

# INCREASING A TENANT'S RENT

In most cases, the rent can increase if at least 12 months have passed since the tenant first moved in or since the tenant's last rent increase.

A landlord must give at least 90 days notice in writing of any rent increase. The proper forms for this notice (Form N1, N2 or N3) are available from the Board.

The Ontario Government sets the rent increase guideline each year.

It based on the Consumer Price Index.

Each year, the Government announces the guideline by August 31st for rent increases that will take effect on or after January 1st of the following year.

A guideline rent increase does not need to be approved by the Board.

However, a landlord must get approval from the Board before they can charge an increase above the guideline.

A landlord can apply to the Board for an increase above the guideline. If the landlord's costs for municipal taxes and charges, and utilities (such as fuel, electricity or water) have increased significantly. The landlord has done significant repairs or renovations (these are called capital expenditures).

The landlord has operating costs for security services performed by persons who are not employees of the landlord. Rent increases for capital expenditures or security services cannot be more than 3% above the guideline each year.

If the landlord justifies an increase that is more than 3% above the guideline, the gain can take over three years, at a rate of up to 3% above the guideline per year.

For increases in the cost of municipal taxes and charges, and utilities, there is no limit on the amount of rent increase that can be approved.

The landlord and tenant can agree to a rent increase above the guideline if they agree that the landlord will do major repairs or renovations. Purchase new equipment for the rental unit, or add a new service for the tenant.

This agreement must be in writing. The proper form for this agreement (Form N10) is available from the Board.

The highest increase that can agree to is 3% above the guideline.

The landlord and tenant make this agreement; the landlord does not need to apply to the Board for approval of the increase.

A tenant has five days after signing this agreement to change their mind and tell their landlord, in writing, that they no longer agree to the rent increase.

Capital expenditure fully paid for; this only applies to tenants who are still living in the same rental unit.

They were living in when the Board approved the rent increase based on capital expenditure. The municipal property tax is reduced by more than the prescribed percentage, resulting in an automatic rent reduction.

# LANDLORD'S RESPONSIBILITIES

A Landlord's primary responsibility is to provide a safe and live able dwelling. The dwelling should include:
A landlord has to keep the rental property in a good state of repair.
A landlord must obey all health, safety, housing and maintenance standards, as set out in any Provincial laws or municipal bylaws.
It is true even if the tenant was aware of the problems when they agreed to rent the unit.
A tenant can apply to the Board if the landlord is not meeting their maintenance obligations.
If the Board agrees that the landlord is not meeting their maintenance obligations, there are some remedies the Board can order. Example the Board can request tenant not have to pay some or all of the rent until the landlord does the repairs. That the landlord cannot increase the rent for the rental unit until any severe maintenance problems fixed.
Weather and waterproofing systems

A working plumbing system
Hot and cold running water
A working heating system
A working electrical system
No infestations of insects and rodents
Sufficient trash cans
Floors, stairways and railings in good repair
Natural lighting in every room
Working windows or proper mechanical ventilation
Safe emergency exits
Working security locks at the main entrance
Working security devices on windows
Working smoke detectors

# LANDLORD'S RIGHTS

Every Landlord has the right to expect a Tenant to
follow the general and legal terms of the Rental
Agreement. As well as tenancy laws that are
established by each Province. The following are the
most standard legal terms found in a Rental
Agreement:
Amount of rent, date due and length of the rental
term
Maintenance and cleanliness of dwelling
Respect the rights of neighbours
Tenant to pay the cost of repairs due to neglect or
damage

# A TENANT'S RESPONSIBILITIES

A tenant must keep their rental unit clean, up to the standard that most people would consider ordinary or usual cleanliness.

A tenant must repair or pay for the repair of any damage to the rental property caused by the tenant, the tenant's guest or another person who lives in the rental unit.

It includes damage to the tenant's unit, as well as any common area such as a hallway, elevator, stairway, and driveway or parking area.

It does not matter whether the damage was done on purpose or by not being careful enough - the tenant is responsible. However, the tenant is not responsible for repairing damage caused by normal "wear and tear." For example, if the carpet has become worn after years of regular use, the tenant would not have to replace the carpet.

A landlord can apply to the Board if the tenant has not repaired any damage.

If the Board agrees that the tenant should be held responsible for the damage, the Board can order the tenant to pay the cost of repairing the damage or even evict the tenant.

A tenant should not withhold any part of the rent, even if the tenant feels that maintenance is poor or a necessary repair has not done.

A tenant could evict if they withhold rent without getting approval from the Board.

# EDUCATION FOR LANDLORD & TENANT

In many cases, a Landlord and Tenant can become adversaries when there is a lack of knowledge regarding rights and responsibilities.

It often results in a Tenant leaving the Landlord stuck with unpaid rental fees and damaged rental property.

A loss of income, stress, hassle and other unpleasant experiences are the result of many such instances which are unnecessary and avoidable.

Of course, there are other reasons for discontent with either one party or the other such as lack of respect, cooperation, cleanliness.

To minimize or alleviate the possibility of these unnecessary problems, it is incumbent upon the landlord to educate himself and the Tenant.

When both Landlord & Tenant know the rules, play by the rules and respect the rules, the Tenant and Landlord experience is a much more pleasant and profitable one.

www.tenantsinfo.com is a website that has designed for the benefit of both Landlord & Tenant.

It is not enough for a Landlord or Tenant to know their rights & responsibilities; he/she should also know the rights & responsibilities of the other party. This scenario will likely eliminate many problems in your rental business.

Take it upon yourself as a Successful Landlord to educate yourself and your Tenant to the best of your ability.
Have your Tenant review the website as part of the lease or tenancy agreement; this will save you time, money and sleepless nights.

# VITAL SERVICES

A landlord cannot shut off or interfere with the supply of any of the following vital services to a tenant's rental unit:
Heat (from September 1st to June 15th)
Electricity
Fuel (such as natural gas or oil)
Hot or cold water

# ASSIGNING A TENANCY AND SUBLETTING

A tenant may be able to transfer their right to occupy the rental unit to someone else.
It is called an assignment. An assignment new person takes the place of the tenant, but all the terms of the rental agreement stay the same.
Sublet occurs when a tenant moves out of the rental unit, lets another person live there for a period, but returns to live in the unit before the tenancy ends.

In a sublet, the terms of the rental agreement and the landlord-tenant relationship do not change. A tenant must have the landlord's approval for an assignment or a sublet, but, in either case, the landlord must have a good reason for refusing. Rules about special tenancies

Some tenants do not have the right to assign their tenancy or sublet. Example, a tenant who is a superintendent, or a tenant who lives in subsidized, public or non-profit housing, or in housing provided by an educational institution where the tenant works or is a student.

# SECURITY DEPOSITS

For the last month's rent, a landlord needs to reimburse the tenant for the interest on that money. The Federal government normally lists the interest rate that determines the amount that you owe the tenant.

The government will also list the maximum level of the rental increase.

Ontario is one of the few provinces in Canada where it's illegal to ask for a damage or security deposit.

# KEYS REPLACEMENT

The landlord should change the locks after one tenant moves out, and a new one moves in.
Consider using the smart key system in the long term it will cost less you have to reprogram the lock to use different keys. So you do not have to remove the hardware.
Landlord nor the tenant can change the lock on any door giving entry to the dwelling without consent from the other.

# EVICTION

There are some other reasons for eviction that are not related to what the tenant has done or not done.
For example, the landlord wants the rental unit for their use or the use of an immediate family member or a caregiver.
The landlord agreed to sell the property the purchaser wants all or part of the property for their use or immediate family member or a caregiver.
The landlord plans significant repairs or renovations that require a building permit and vacant possession.
The landlord intends to demolish the rental property.
The eviction process can be very challenging and costly; try to avoid it as much as possible.
Be knowledgeable of the law for your province or State.

Have a copy of the Landlord and Tenancy Acts

# HIRE A HANDYMAN

The question to ask before hiring a handyman
What are your abilities and experience?
How long have you been working as a handyman?
Are there any tasks that you may not feel comfortable performing?
How do you charge for your services?
Is it by the hour or the ½ hour? Do you charge a minimum rate?
Do you charge for estimates?
Who would be paying for materials for this job?
Do you charge a material markup fee?
Do you charge for travel time?
Do you offer any forms of guarantees or warranties on the work you perform?
What types of local registration, licenses and insurance do you have?
Can you provide proof of contractor liability insurance?
Do you have any references?
A handyman should have the necessary knowledge plumbing, electrical, carpentry and general repair skills and someone who is accessible mobile and has the proper set of equipment.

They should be reliable, honest and responsible. You are entrusting them with your tenant's keys to enter their rental units unsupervised.

Length of Time to Keep Tenants Records after Termination of Lease. Whether the tenant or property owner/Landlord terminates, the lease agreement records should be kept for 2-3 years after.

Add a summary note to the close tenant file will help with reference years later

Sometimes potential property owner/landlord looking for reference goes back to at least two years looking for tenant payment history.

# STAGING

Home staging and home decorating are not the same.

When you decorate your home, you do so with a flair for what you like.

Home staging should be done in such a way as to make your rental unit more appealing to a prospective client.

When should you consider staging your rental unit? When it is taking too long to get the unit rented, or in a high rental vacancy area, to showcase the unit potential features.

Rental property staging is all about creating an illusion for the potential tenants.

In general, colours that have more of a blue base are perceived to be on the cool side.

Colours in the red or orange groups lean to the warm side.

Colours can create a mood.

Warm colours tend to exude a more energetic mood.

Cooler colours can have a calming effect.

Before you choose a paint colour, get a sense of whether your rental space has a "warm" feel or a "cool" feel.

Also, consider a visit to a local paint and design store. Their consultants and designers can assist you in determining the warmth or coolness of your rental space.

They can give you colour suggestions that you might not have considered.

There are only three primary colours yellow, red and blue because no other colours can be mixed to make any of the primary colours.

The three secondary colours, purple, green and orange mean two colours mixed to make them.

Neutral colours such as brown, white, gray and black these are most likely to appeal to most potential tenants.

When potential tenants see neutral walls, they can gravitate more easily to see their furniture and accessories in that space.

While freshly painted walls have a huge benefit to gain potential tenants, use of neutral colours is your safest way to go to appeal to the masses.

Allow as much natural light into the rental unit as much as possible.

Window coverings using sheer drapes instead of heavy and dark coverings.

Open blinds, curtains and shades will allow maximum light in the home.

Update any outdated or dim light, old light fixtures with brighter lights.

Ensure all light bulbs are operable a bright well-lit space will be emotionally uplifting, while at the same time make space feel larger.

The illusion of a rental unit having more space is essential.

A staging portfolio of a two-bedroom apartment The inside of the apartment looks beautiful, but the washroom was very dull, and potential tenants lost interest. I took the owner of this apartment through as a prospective tenant. Then to give me the reason why she would or would not rent this apartment. She was able to see through her potential tenant's eyes.

Upgrade the Washroom

This apartment rents about three days later after the upgrade. The washroom became a conversation piece for every potential tenant. The upgrade cost less than a $100.00

# CHAPTER 6 PROPERTY MANAGER AND OTHER SERVICES

Too complex for you then hire a Property Manager When do you hire a Property Manager; have two or more properties, lack people skills, if you live far away from the rental property. Do not have the time to manage the property and sometimes base on the size of the Residential Income Property. When you are buying an apartment building at the onset, you need a Property Manager for commercial Income Property; you need one due to the complexity of those leasing contract. Base on the type of business your leasing your property for there are different types of lease options to use, e.g., percentage, straight and overage. The advantage of a Percentage lease from the tenant's point of view is that it is a long-term lease with a minimum fair rental. Obligating the tenant to pay additional amounts only when business volume justifies an increase. The owner is allowed to share in the increasing value of business volume and the location. Straight percentage the rental rate is based solely on a percentage of the gross income of the business, with no minimum guaranteed the rent.

Overage leases are sometimes called minimum guaranteed percentage and are more beneficial to the owner. Payments of coverage rent may be made monthly and then usually adjusted on an annual basis.

Hire a Property Manager base on their due diligence. Sometimes landlords do not like to hear the truth because they prefer not to make the necessary changes for long-term prevention due to cost. New owners buy houses with basement apartment with small windows that not up to fire code. As a Property Manager, you have to tell them because their Real Estate Agent who sell them that property did not do their due diligence. You need to have two exits meaning a window and a door that in case of a fire, the tenant cannot get out the door, they can use the window as an escape route.

Many new income property owners are misleading about the investment property by agents said you could make 1500 dollar per month for that three bedrooms apartment. It's rundown need a facelift, dirty. He/she got their commission and said thank you nice doing business with you.

The Property Manager shows up and has to be the bearer of the bad news, but Agent Tom told me that I could rent it as it is. Now you have to send them to detox from Agent Tom drugs and bring them back to reality.

Mr. Owner, you are a potential tenant would you live in this apartment "no" so why would you expect your tenant to live in it. You spend all that you have on buying this income property with no contingency funds to pay for necessary upgrades, getting a cleaning service, a painter. Well, Mr. Owner, you will have to put in some sweat equity to bring it up to a rentable standard. Income Property Owners the apartment you show must have a good reflection because that will be your tenant's perception of you. If you give then a poor representation of you that will be the type of tenants you will attract. Property Manager don't be afraid to walk away from those properties every client that comes to you will not be your client. You have an image to uphold.

# REAL PROPERTY MANAGEMENT SCENARIOS

This property owner was already in the income property business and decided to buy another property out of her city. Now people are doing all of these credit check, employment history, bank statement, income statement, previous landlord reference. For potential tenants to get an apartment to live. Her remarks were so profound said all of those pre-screening being done to get information is great. The reality you have to go with your gut feelings to choose a good tenant. She was correct.

I have seen tenants with poor credit score but always pay their rent without any problems. That kind of pre-screen system would put good tenants who do not have that perfect credit scores on the street to live. I spoke to an income property owner who had a townhouse rented to a Mortgage Broker. Who comes with an excellent credit score and a good reference from the previous Landlord was not paying his rent.

Here is a case where two sisters with a baby looking for an apartment they were staying with a friend. Needed their space, have no credit history works as a House Cleaner in private houses. The friend that they lived with said he would be a co-signer for them, but he is not moving to this apartment. Here comes the egotistical mentor ask about the unit rental he was a mentor for the property owner and the Property Manager the deal explained to him. The owner knowing the status of the potential tenants agree to accept them. The mentor tells the Property Manager to say to the property owner to reject the deal because the co-signer is not living in the apartment. If they are in default, it will difficult to hold him accountable.

The owner maxes out all her resources to buy the property and mortgage is due a month later. It was a two-bedroom apartment at $1000 per month. The message of the mentor was related to the owner, her response was is he going to pay my mortgage, and she did not reject it.

The Property Manager kept the potential tenants in the loop about the mentoring advice to reject their lease agreement. They were happy they got the apartment and every month paid their rent with no problem.

Here is another tenant moving in a two bedrooms basement apartment the first of the month was on Sunday ask if they could move in on Saturday instead. They had friends and family available to help. The owner agrees because the apartment was empty. The Property Manager did a second inspection of the unit to ensure it would be ready for moving the next day. Still, there were a few things not completed by the contractor; a message left for the owner and the contractor about it. One of the problems was the closet in their bedroom rod not put up. The contractor went away for the week and back in town until Monday, and the owner said they have to wait until then. Tenant getting very angry to have nowhere to put her clothing owner comment was I have a horrible feeling about this one. Why is the tenant so upset about they moved in a day early without any extra cost. If they had moved in on the first of the month, the apartment would not have been ready for them? The tenant had a good relationship with the Property Manager tried to merge the gap between the owner and the tenant with little success. The owner was new to the income property world and needed to understand she was providing a service.

The tenant was her client; there is a level of expectation that she will need to meet. The owner already made a negative statement about tenant behaviour, and it became alive; they did not have a good tenant and landlord relationship. Every tenant has a different level of expectation; human management is one of the most challenging situations.

When owners bring a spirit of dishonest into a deal, it plays out in their tenants. This situation, a property owner hires a Property Manager to find a tenant for their rental units but still trying to show the apartments on their own. If they rent, it would not have to pay the Property Manager. Property Managers take note of this situation and make sure a clause in your agreement. To ensure if the owner fined the tenant during the time they retain your services, you still get your pay. Property Manager new tenants for one of the unit pre-screen done accept the tenant, no pet allowed it was in the lease agreement and told verbally to the tenant. The tenant said he had no pet after he moves in with a pet's farm.

The previous landlord said the tenant was great has no problems paying his rent. See, even though pre-screen done it did not tell you who this tenant is until they move in when one landlord wants to get rid of a bad tenant.

He or she gives the potential landlord great report because they want them to transfer to someone else and no longer their problem. In this case, the owners became the tenant friends stop by having a drink with them. Giving the tenant the message, we are friends now it is okay to do whatsoever you want and then expect the Property Manager to fix the problem. Landlord/Owner should maintain a good relationship with their tenants but not be their best friend.

How many landlords/owners have a problem tenant and would tell potential landlords/owners that is a problematic tenant.

This situation, a tenant in an apartment not paying rent for four months, now the owner hires a Property Manager to handle this case. The tenant is on social assistance; there is no possibility of him gaining those back rent. Property Manager discusses with the owner to make the tenant and offer instead of going through the very costly eviction process. Gave her a month to move, and the owner will give up his rights to sue her for the back rent. She accepts it the case closed. In this case, the likelihood of him recouping the back rent is nil. Therefore, he would just be spending money that he did not have due to the unpaid rents for months by another tenant in the one-bedroom suite.

Here is a tenant Sue living in a one-bedroom apartment with a balcony on the second floor in a low rise apartment. She had a basket on the balcony someone climb over and stole it. She became very concern about her safety because the balcony door is an old plywood door that someone can kick in easily. She wrote a letter to the Landlord asking for an apartment on a higher floor, but he did not respond to her. She went out and looked for another apartment and informs him that she will be moving in 30 days. Then he shows up to tell her he will give her an apartment on a higher floor; she rejects it because she already got a new apartment. Then he begins to argue that she needs to provide him with sixty days notice. She had a law book give necessary information on the different topics; she looks under the tenancy act to find out how to deal with the situation.

She sent him back the previous letter she had issued to him with no response. She also added another one is addressing her concern for her safety and being sleep deprived. She informed him that it would cause difficulty in her job. The landlord waited for almost the last week before beginning to show the apartment for rent. Sue perceived he went to his Lawyer, and he told him to rent the apartment because he would not be able to win that case. It was the clause Sue found in the law book to break her lease without any penalty.

If you live in an apartment and a club built after, and it begins to disturb you as a tenant, you can break the lease and leave without giving sixty days notice. That tenant could not foresee that a nightclub would be built to disturb her. If she had moved after the nightclub established, she would not have that clause to break the least.

Here is a story of a very greedy landlord/illegal basement apartment. He had four-bedroom apartments in the basement. The layout was two washrooms and a tiny kitchen with one regular size fridge to share with four people. No living room area and two of the rooms are illegal because it has no windows. Two rooms were tiny. The landlord stated they destroy his place, so he had to evict the previous tenants. He was renting each room individually $450 -$500 would earn about $1950 per month on the basement. He could make it into a three-bedroom apartment with a living and dining and rent it to a family for about $1550 per month. He wants to make more money, but it takes him and one tenant who know the fire code and call the city and close it down. That was not a safe place, and it did not have proper ventilation, which can cause tenants to get frustrated, depress, angrily.

Then the landlord wonders why they damage his place, toxic air, and tenants breathing could be possible to cause them to do strange things.

Here is a real tenant tribunal court case an associate share with me. A tenant with three small kids live in an apartment within a house she was paying her rent and all the utilities, and another tenant lives in the basement apartment. The landlord files an N12 to terminate the tenancy to reclaim the space for personal usage. The tenant asks the landlord to work with her and give her some time to move. It was in winter, and her children are in school, and it is difficult to move with three small children in the middle of winter. He did not want to work with her. He took advice from a Real Estate Agent to proceed with the N12 form. They went to court, and the judgement was in favour of the tenant. She gets to live in the apartment for two months free $1200 per month, Landlord has to pay $650 towards her moving cost. Pending she moves within the time frame, the judge gave her, and he also has to pay the full court cost of $190. It cost the landlord $3240 for not working with the tenant as she had requested. Some landlord tries to use this N12 to terminate a tenancy in bad faith. Knowingly they want to get rid of the tenant related to the conflict; there is enormous find to misrepresent the use of the space. Since September 1, 2017, the rules changed for all landlords in Ontario who give notice for the termination of a residential tenancy.

They require the unit for their use — for an immediate family member, defined as the owner's parent, spouse, child, and spouse's parent or child. Landlords still required to give their tenant at least 60 days' written notice to the end of the term or rent period using the Landlord and Tenant Board Form N12. Make sure you are using the current form N12 — updated on September 1, 2017.

# NEW CRITERIA

Effective September 1, 2017, amendments to the Residential Tenancies Act, 2006 (RTA) now require the following:

Landlords are required to pay the tenant one month's rent compensation. Offer the tenant an acceptable alternate rental unit when terminating a tenancy based on own use.

The landlord or immediate family member requiring the rental unit must occupy the unit for a minimum of twelve months.

Landlords giving this notice must be an individual who owns the rental unit in whole or in part.

It is now an offense under the RTA for a landlord to knowingly end a tenancy by giving notice in bad faith. A conviction for this offense can result in a fine of up to $25,000 for an individual.

Landlord Acted in Bad Faith Towards Tenant .

Bad faith occurs when a landlord gives a tenant a Form N12 notice for own use as a way to end the tenancy because of other issues.

It means the landlord or their immediate family members, does not have a genuine intention to move into the unit to live there themselves. A tenant may be causing damage in the unit or disturbing other tenants, and address the situations. The landlord serves the tenant with a Form N12 because the landlord believes this is the least combative way to ask the tenant to leave. It is a common mistake made by landlords, which can lead to severe consequences.

If a landlord gave a notice of termination in bad faith, if within one year:

1. The landlord does not allow advertising the rental unit for rent or the building that contains the rental unit, for sale.

2. The landlord should not enter into a tenancy agreement in respect of the rental unit with someone else other than the former tenant.

3. Takes any steps to convert the rental unit, or the building containing the rental unit, to use for a purpose other than residential premises.

What is compensation for the tenant and when must it be paid?

Section 48.1 of the RTA requires that compensation equal to one month's rent paid to the tenant before the termination date specified in the N12 notice. Landlords may apply with the LTB to obtain an order terminating the tenancy under the notice before the termination date. Landlords are encouraged to file their L2 application before the termination date to ensure the payment of compensation to the tenant becomes part of the LTB order.

If a landlord is found by the Landlord and Tenant Board to have acted in bad faith, the landlord could be ordered to pay the following:

All or any portion of any increased rent that the former tenant has incurred or will incur for one year after vacating the rental unit.

Reasonable out-of-pocket moving, storage, or other like expenses that the former tenant has incurred or will incur.

An order that the landlord pays a fine to the Board, e.g., the court fee in total.

In conclusion, these changes are intended to increase protection for tenants and discourage landlords from unlawfully evicting tenants, whether to convert to a short-term rental or rent at a higher rate.

# OTHER SERVICES

You hire a cleaning service to clean your income property before the potential tenant move in; you need to understand what type of cleaning required. A lot of owners/landlords want to be cheap because they do not want to spend the money to do a proper clean. When you hire a cleaning person privately, that is okay, but you now become their employer if any injury to that person under the employer standard, you are liable for that employee. Do you know why cleaning company charges more it is to take that liability away from you as the client and insure their employees? Most of those properties need what's called a deep clean, especially if another tenant had just moved out.

Your new tenant does not want to come and live on the previous tenant dirt.

Let's understand the first rule not because a person clean their home/apartment does not mean they are qualified to clean an income property.

You can hire your next-door neighbour or yourself to clean to save money but did you save?

When your new tenant moves in and finds a lot of areas not done properly or at all.

Areas prone to miss are inside cupboards, behind the stove and fridge The big deal is when your new tenant move in your message to them, my lips said I care about you, but my heart said I do not care, want to get your money.

The visible areas represent your lips service that they can see. The hidden field is your heart that closed under a mass of tissues they cannot see; speak more volume. The first impression is the lasting impression, and you will not have the chance to make that first impression again. Let 's look back at the story in the real Property Manager Scenarios where the new tenants move in had no place to hang her clothing and the owner attitude. They never establish a good tenant and landlord relationship. Having an income suite allows you to take cheques to the bank for a very long time it set the right tone for your tenant from the beginning. It is not just about collecting rents; there is a certain degree of work that needs to put to be a success. No one goes to work and receive a paycheque from the boss without doing their job. So why do you think it would be any different being a property owner/landlord? As property owners/landlords here are some terms, you need to get familiar with deep clean, move in or move clean what it entailed in these services. Cleaning is hard work don't always look for discounts if you build a good relationship with your cleaning service provider the discount will come.

As property owners/landlords, how often you use that cleaning service maybe once in a year or longer, they would starve waiting for your business. Find out what the service cost without you providing the cleaning products and if you provide the cleaning products, what is the cost also.

If it cost the same or close to, then let the company supply the products. A new construction cleaning is different from a move out cleaning. The newly constructed income suite is more dust focus. They do not wipe freshly painted walls, appliances are new just a quick wipe in the fridge and microwave. Move out or move in clean, required the same attention and most of the time is a deep clean. To give you a greater understanding of what goes into cleaning an income suite see below Deep Cleaning Empty Income Suite chart.

Deep Cleaning Empty Income Suite
Cabinet cleaning included Linen Closet
Wipe Walls if not freshly painted
Clean Behind Washer/Dryer
Removed Cobwebs from all areas
All Bathrooms Cleaned
Clean Under Bathroom Sink
Clean Under Kitchen Sink
Vacuum under Furniture Cushions (if it is a furnished suite)
Clean Refrigerator/Freezer
Clean Inside Kitchen Cabinets
All Kitchen counters wiped
Outside of all Appliances Wiped
Microwave Cleaned In and Outsid
Wash/Dusted Baseboards
Trash Cans Empty and Clean Inside and Outside
Clean Oven (Self-cleaning please turn on the night before)

Oven In and Outside

Clean Behind Oven/Refrigerator (Top of The Fridge Included)

All Window Sills Dusted/wiped (interior)

All Mirrors Cleaned

Complete Dust (interior)

Clean Stovetop, Oven, Grill and range hood

Clean cupboard interior and exterior

Vacuum and Mop floor

Dust Blinds For Example- All the work are needed to be done very cleanly & in an efficient way by an Expert.

Vacuuming Carpet Cleaning

If there is carpet in the suite might need to call a Professional Carpet Cleaner to steam.

You hire a contractor; to understand how the process works; you want your income property to look beautiful but not breaking the bank doing it. Have some understanding of how the renovation process work is excellent.

Changing the layout of the design for a kitchen or reroute a bedroom to another location of the floor plan, moving plumbing pipes and adding a washroom all cost a lot more money.

Maintain the original floor plans refurbish your kitchen and bathroom cupboards and change the handles. If it is wood floors varnish it changes pipe faucets; bathtub can restore, paint unit.

Spend money buying new inexpensive energy appliances you can save yourself a lot of money. Building a new income suite do not do a custom kitchen go to a place like Home Depot Store and buy a premade kitchen. The engineered hardwood still look great but cost a fraction of the price. Purchase energy-saving appliance but shop around for savings. Durability and cost-effectiveness are best for an income suite because, over the life of the suite, you might have different occupants. Who does not have the same attachment to it as you do? They would not handle the unit the same way and also take into account wear and tear over the years. When does a property owner put in dishwasher, washer, and dryer in a unit in executive rentals and high-end apartments?

In the regular apartments, it might cost you a lot, and the rental income does not justify it on that unit. Coin laundry is suitable for investment properties, especially if utilities included.

# CHAPTER 7 BE YOUR OWN BEST FINANCIAL ADVISER

Be your financial adviser meaning understanding where your money invest how the investment market works. The know-how of why major banks do not collapse during stock market crashes and know when to shift your money in a financial market downturn. Educate yourself on the Financial Market by attending seminars, reading reliable publications, e.g., Business Week, Fortune Magazine and The Wall Street Journal. Having financial knowledge of the investment market, you can cut out the middleman in some of your investment and save on some of those fees. A Financial Advisor misled me before he sold me a Whole Life Insurance without letting me know that there were other options. He earns a more significant commission. It sounds right at the time because I did not know, so I trusted that Financial Advisor. After I read a few books on Life Insurance realize bought the wrong policy it had cash built up a component and life insurance on the plan, paying $100.00 per month.

Twenty years old when I purchased this policy. Already paid about $6000 into the plan, but the statements come every year but never spend the time to read it.

So I understood more about Life Insurance now, so open the statement and read found out my $6000 only value about $4000. I call the

Financial Advisor in to ask him why he sold me that Whole Life Insurance policy begins to justify it by using the cash component aspect. Then he starts to attack one of the Authors from one of the books I read. He knew he did not do his due diligence but refused to accept it. The knowledge gained makes me powerful, transfer my funds from his company to another Financial Institution.

Decided to be a Financial Advisor to change the way people get financial advice so that they would understand the pro and con of investment. I had a mutual fund and life insurance license years ago and used to sell funds to people. I had to do my due diligence to get to know my clients and their comfort level to invest.

Many clients do not want to take any risk I would give them in guaranteed funds like GIC, money market account with a lower return on their money. They would not lose their money.

Then you have the clients who like to take a risk which gives them a higher rate of return, but they could lose their money.

I thought clients how to diversify their funds to reduce the risk of losing all their money. Explain a lot of jargon to my clients about the funds before I would get them to invest.

The success of the fund is base on the Portfolio Managers experience, their net asset value. Treasury bonds, bills and notes are loans to the Canadian and U.S. government if they go out of business the world would end. It is considered a safe investment; they will always be able to make interest payments.

A bond investor protected over a shareholder in the likelihood the fund company runs into financial difficulties. It still has a legal obligation to make timely payments of interest and principal to the bond investor, but the company has no similar obligation to pay dividends to shareholders. When you purchase shares of a company through a broker, you pay a brokerage fee.  These fees over time can take a considerable portion of your returns.

Have a mindset that no one will ever pay you, your self-worth. Understand yourself worth is vitally important to build wealth. The system of this world is designed to keep you in abject poverty but do not maintain a poverty mindset.

Government is organized not to make people wealthy. The government was established to organize society.

In lots of countries, the government encourages people to save for their retirement benefits; they sometimes give them a tax break to do so. In Canada, have RRSP (Register Retirement Saving Plan). An RRSP is a retirement saving plan that you establish, that we register, and to which you or your spouse or common-law partner contributed.

Deductible RRSP contributions can be used to reduce your taxable income. The income you earn in the RRSP is usually exempt from tax as long as the funds remain in the plan; you have to pay tax when you withdraw funds from the plan. As a first time home buyer, you are allowed to borrow money from your RRSP for a period, but you have to pay it back. When you withdraw funds from your RRSP, it becomes taxable income, the larger the amount withdrawn the more taxes you will pay. The front end, the government gives you a tax break to invest your money in RRSP at the back end, is taxable. You can receive income from an RRSP by transfer the funds to RRIF (registered retirement income fund) up to age 71. Starting in the year after your RRIF establish you will receive a minimum amount each year using a predetermined formula based on the value of the RRIF and your age. You can also use your RRSP funds to purchase an annuity. Annuities offer a guaranteed income for life or a specified period.

There is no such thing as retirement benefits, and the government will have a shortfall in paying it out; so you are encouraged to save your money through an RRSP. When you contribute to your RRSP, the government takes the money and invest it and can earn 30% or more on it give you a 10 or 12 % interest rate of return.

For those who are contributing to a pension now is what is presently using for people getting pensions. You could be the poorest of the poorest but, maintain a success mindset, that where you are not where you will remain.

Other funds can purchase for wealth building stocks, bank funds, health, mutual funds but the diversity of your portfolios is significant to decrease volatility or lose all of your money. Real Estate is still the best investment. To get a better rate of return on your money, investing in high-risk investments tends to yield the best return. Know what your risk level is to invest — owning your own business to generate better cash flow and leave generational wealth. Investment businesses good to invest in Nursing Home, Daycare, constructions, Health and Wellness, Banks. Do your research before you agree to invest, hire a Financial Manager who has your best interest. Not someone only wants to gain more significant income for them self.

Personal RRSP investment story. In Canada, we had up until March 1 to buy RRSP to claim on the prior year Income Tax to get the tax-deductible for that year. Somewhere in 2000 the last day March 1 went into the bank to buy some mutual funds for my RRSP, knew the funds wanted to buy. The Mutual Rep told me could not purchase the funds like that. They have to complete an assessment form to see if that is the fund I should be investing.

Told her understood the use of her assessment but am not a new investor, and it would not change my mind about what funds I want to invest. I told her to draft me a consent that said I decline all of this assessment, and I will sign it, she refused and called the Bank Manager.

The Bank Manager told me that could not purchase the funds there this is my regular branch. I went home to purchase the funds online without having to do an assessment. Here were these two women trying to control how I invest my money because of a walk into the bank with too much knowledge about the mutual fund. Those two funds wanted to purchase were doing very well at the time. A system design to keep us in poverty that is the reason be your own Financial Adviser is key to your success.

# TEACH YOUR CHILDREN THE VALUE OF MONEY

Too often, children do not know the value of money they see their parents go off to work but do not know how hard they work for that dollar. They ask their parents for stuff mom or dad give them the money, and off they go to make that purchase. Parents need to bring children to an understanding that it is not easy to make money, and that it should treat with respect.

Sometimes parents buy a lot of toys that gathering dust because they have too much. That toy was their favourite until they get a new one; sometimes teach them to share with other less fortunate children. The emphasis should be put on schooling and education and not stuff. Allow them to have summer jobs and teach them how to save money from chores, jobs and money gifts given to them. If your children see you as a parent careless with money, they will think it is okay for them to do the same. It is a generational cycle that goes from one generation to another. As a child growing up with my grandaunt, I did not ask for a lot of stuff, but I expected to get it each time upon request. She did not give me every time would request, so I thought she was stingy. Today I appreciate her; she was teaching me the valuable lesson of living within my means because I would not get everything at all times.

Let's look at a child, Dave, at the age of five getting $10.00 per week for allowance, teaching him how to save by using the jar system. In jar number one, is his tithes and offering of $1.50, second jar- entertainment $4.00, third jar- money to save $4.50. When the jar with savings gets to $100.00, take him to the bank and open an account for him. He can begin to gain interest on the money. For the year he will have in saving $218.00. Some people teach their children to be poor; they will tell them to become a Doctor or a Lawyer; they will always have a job for life.

Being a Doctor or a Lawyer is a great profession, but they need to go beyond a job for life. Add to their profession some significant investments a few income properties, stock. Who wants to work for life so you will not be able to enjoy what you accomplish?

# WILL AND ESTATE PLANNING

A will in testament is a legal document one that relates to the disposition of one's personal property or assets. A will cannot enforce until the testator died. Testator: a person who makes a will, a person who has died leaving a valid will. It is essential to have a will in testament upon your death your assets can dispose of to your family or friend, charity without any issues.

Today some people are not honest to divide up your estate honestly without fighting.

When you make a will, you need to appoint an executor that upon your death, the execution of your will can carry out effectively? You should have more than one executor for some reason the first executor becomes incapable then the second executor can step in as a replacement. An executor can be your Lawyer, a friend, family by law they are entitled to get paid to preside over your will. To preside over a will can become very difficult in some case where some family might decide to contest the will.

If there are a lot of assets, and it has to go through probate.

Your will must state what your wishes. Here is a scenario wife died and her will said all her estate goes to her husband and upon his death the children inherit it. During this time husband got married again and moved a new wife in the family house that suppose to go to the children. The status of a family home is changed to a matrimonial home again. If the second wife in a divorce can fight for that home under the family law, so where does it leave the children inheritance.

Probate: the official proving of a will as authentic or valid in a probate court

If you are a wealthy person upon your death, taxes have to pay upon your estate, having life insurance to cover the cost is wise.

So your beneficiary would not lose a significant amount of it covering the cost. In the interim have young children and need some quick cash to take care of their wellbeing life insurance is the option; it is redeemable tax-free.

When doing your estate planning and no longer able to take care of yourself, you need to have a Power of Attorney for both Financial and Personal Care. To act as a legal representative in both areas, and they can be two separate for each. Appoint two extra people for Financial and Personal Care as a backup. In case anyone become incapable, the second person can step in.

Someone you can trust implicitly and that they know what your wishes are to execute it effectively. That person can be a spouse, family member or friend. A Power of Attorney is only
activated when that person deemed incapable of making a financial decision by a medical Doctor.
A medical Doctor deems granny incapable of making a financial decision that is only for financial, but she still has her rights to decide on her care.
She lives in a Nursing Home; they are trying to feed or giving her medication.
She refused they cannot force her they can still try to encourage her to take it but still refused they have to respect her wishes.
I went to a seminar one day on the topic of Power of Attorney for both Financial and Personal Care the presenter use this scenario. If I was cognitively alert at midnight, and you did not show up with that consent for me to sign. It does not mean I cannot decide on my care. Having a living will for medical directives is excellent in the process of you become incapable of making a decision. It speaks for you the doctor will follow it, and no family can override it once a copy is made available to the medical team. Mary, the daughter, wants her mother on a life support system. Her living will say "no" life support machine; the doctor will not put her on it. A daughter was making medical decisions for her mother before the living will show up.

All the medical directives were giving before gets a veto by the Living Will if not compatible with it. If you have a young family, make the decision who; will take care of your children in case of the death of both parents. Heard a Politician said as they thought about who would take care of their children in the case both of them died.

Could not find a suitable person in their family or friends. They make the decision to travel in separate cars, and even if they are flying to the same country, they take a different flight. In conclusion, Will and Estate Planning is imperative for everyone, no matter how great or small your asset or estate.

# CONCLUSION

When you think Real Estate see the generational wealth that keeps replicating for many generations. Remember what makes news is publicity, and people strive on it. A news report said the housing market is down. It creates a buzz then some people begin to second guess buying Real Estate out of fear of losing their money. How many reports have we heard talks about the number of people purchase Real Estate frequently? Look around us in Toronto and other areas how many residential buildings are building Condo's, Townhouses, and Houses. People always need places to live, but the most effective is having an income suite even in your principal residence. If you are unable to buy a separate income investment property or you can have both. We are birthing more Real Estate Agents more than ever there is a demand. Banks still lending money to buy Real Estate. A large percentage of the Stock Market and Mutual Funds invest in Real Estate. Real Estate is a tangible investment, and an income property occupied by tenants will always ride out any inflation in the housing market.

You can use the income from your Real Estate investment to fund your retirement, dream vacations, pay for your children educations and remain a wealth-building tool for many generations, with a more significant financial gain.

Moving your common-law spouse or spouse (woman or man) into your principal residence changes the status of to a matrimonial home.

Get a Lawyer to give you proper advice on the terms and agreement in which you move a common-law spouse or spouse. Your residence had before the establishment of the relationship. After several years that relationship breaks up. It becomes a part of the divorce or separation settlement under the family law, wherein you will have to give them a part of the whole house. Be smart do not get caught in the emotional trap of love and lose your asset. List all your asset had before the relationship. Common-law spouse moves in with a lease agreement they have to pay rent until you establish the stability of the relationship. Met a Lawyer who was married as soon as he finishes pay off for the house, his wife asks for a divorce, and the house was a part of her settlement they had children. He had to leave and live in his grandparent's basement.

Having an income property or income suite you are providing a service, your tenants or your clients who pay for the service. Taking cheques to the bank great but treating your tenants with respect is a more significant asset to retain your long-term goals.